AMONG FRIENDS

AMONG FRIENDS

Poems

David Langworthy

This book was printed in the United States of America.

To order additional copies of this book, contact:
Xlibris Corporation
1-888-795-4274
www.Xlibris.com
Orders@Xlibris.com
18198

CONTENTS

PART ONE
Family Feeling

PART TWO
Vivid Ghosts

PART THREE
Falling

PART FOUR
Among Friends

PART FIVE
Fables

PART ONE

Family Feeling

A POET'S NEED

A poet needs no praise or wage,
but anglers to catch his thought:
there's no virtue in a page
till readers fish it out.

FAMILY FEELING

A bruise you forget till you bump it;
a too-muchness; a seldom-enoughness; a need
that urges, yet deforms community;
a knowing so intimate it forgives
in time or too late or, rarely, never;
an invisible connection so secure
that death itself seldom breaks it, but draws
the scattered kin into a formal knot.

Through evolution, revolution, failure,
the family survives. After all,
where else can you get such lasting hurts and helps
or give them so conveniently, so surely?

TILL THE COWS CAME HOME

One hot August day Dad and a friend
worked till noon penning and loading cattle
grown sleek and wild in a river pasture. The end
of their morning's fence-busting chase and battle
found them parched, the beasts as much as the men.
They stopped in the village and parked the bellowing truck
beneath the telephone-exchange, where the township's
Central gossip perched like a scolding wren.
Though they crossed the street for a single beer, such
a thirst as theirs took hours to heal. They clowned it
up with the constable sent to persuade them home.
He joined them instead, as our other ambassadors did.
The cattle and Mrs. McMonagle broadcast our shame,
and I called curses down on my father's head.

Chores were done and supper on the table
when the errant truck came weaving down the road.
I got to the barn as quick as I was able—
soon enough to see the chute explode
as the truck smashed it. We shoved the splintered boards
to the side, the men stumbling and laughing while I
kicked and pushed the pile with puritan force,
not daring yet to trust my fury to words.
The cattle heaved their anguish at the sky,
but balked at walking an inclined plank, of course,
and had to be pushed down it. Once at the tank,
they fought as if for the privilege of drowning.
Ignoring the evils of too little drink
I turned to squelch, if I could, my father's clowning.

"Le's go see what Dot can fix for us—
b'sides a quarrel. Wotthehell! 'Nother
drunk won't faze her. Come on in for jus'
a li'l while," he coaxed, knowing that Mother
would hold her heaviest fire till Jim had gone.
Jim was eager to stay (his fuming frau
could wait for vengeance) but suddenly I took charge
and packed Jim like a leaky sack of grain
into the cab of his truck, not caring how
he swore at me. Riding a sullen surge
of righteousness, I smothered Dad's complaint
in fault-finding silence as we headed
for the house. A very vindictive saint,
I gloated as his gladness slowly faded.

Steaming black coffee, tomato juice,
and angry reproaches turned his stomach at last.
Hunched in the kitchen rocker, the taut thews
of his neck jerking, his knotted hands grasping
his knees, he spilled the afternoon's debauch
into the basin he had grabbed. Now
I felt ashamed truly, not of him
but of my treason. I forced myself to watch
his suffering and achingly to know
in my own pride the sin that exiled Ham.
Though we might try to force it out of mind,
this day would run between us; and neither ever
(or so my shame admonished me) would find
sufficient grace to bridge the sudden river.

But I was wrong. Although the river remained,
in time we built a bridge, and each could cross it
freely to ask or offer a helping hand.
Even at floodstage we never had to close it.
The river had always been pushing underground,
seeking a fault or fall to break through
to open sunlight. Now that we could see
our differences and judge their force, we found
the charity to honor them. I knew
my father at last as a man hopeless for me
to imitate: the happy peace he had made
between his conscience and his desires
could only aggravate my nature's need.
Yet our bridge was a boon that eased my blundering years.

CHRISTMAS THISTLE

We found it lodged against our backyard fence:
a becalmed tumbleweed or Russian thistle,
a bulging armful, but light enough to need
its thorns to keep from being slighted.
We wondered how far this bristly tramp had come
and if it meant to stay with us or catch
the next wind out of town. Then, having neither
a Christmas tree nor money to buy one, we
pretended a witty Providence had left
this prickly proxy to mock our improvidence.
We took the thistle in and gingerly
removed the grass and litter gathered in
its suburban rambles. The myriad brown barbs
were nearly as poignant as our memories
of piney fragrance and green grace. But when
we had the thistle dressed and stood back
to see red globes nested in angel's hair,
we only had one mute misgiving left.
A dear—indeed, extravagant—neighbor came
just then and gave our tacit doubt a voice:
she struck an attitude and shrieked, "How *awf-*
ly clever!" But it was Christmas; we forgave her.
We put the baby's crib beside the "tree."
She watched the shiny spheres as if they were eggs
about to hatch and fill the room with birds
singing joyful carols. Reaching for one,
she pricked her tiny finger on a thorn,
but didn't cry until we ran to save her.

Our tree was still a thistle. Decorations
changed its nature no more than Christ's
sacrifice has mended human nature,
though we do our human best to honor him
at Christmas with celebrations of the grace
he lived and tried to give us. The thistle had
a telling point: more (and less) than emblem
of hope or loss, it meant just what it was.
Able to resist our human wills
with who knows what virtues?—weeds and pests
are here for reasons too obscure (or thorny)
for me to grasp. Nor do I know why we
are here, unless to learn to love and lose
the world that crowns its Advocate with thorns.

Hanford, California, 1956

DEAD TURTLE

Our daughter's turtle, diminutive descendent of
that giant tortoise upon whose back the world once rested,
has joined the angel-turtle chorus. "O love! O love!"
he sings. A pretty fate for one that looked so evil.

Though dull and awkward-seeming on his rock, in water
he was dreadful: he'd plunge on peaceful, sucking snails
to butt and bite and rend them—oh, appalling slaughter
for a little girl to witness! (Or a squeamish father.)

Nor could goldfish, though they might dart and flash like flame,
escape the turtle's jaws. He'd slash their filmy fins
to tatters, then close in for the kill. But who will blame
the turtle? Our daughter might reprove him, but even she

knew he was not to be reformed. Yet, dead, he wins
more tears then ever fell for murdered snails or goldfish.
If I should die so full of unrepented sins
as he, may there be tears and prayers like these for me!

TO MY MUSE

I heard a cynic say, "A poet's muse
must never wed her wooer. If she does
she falls from grace and into slavery.
No more has she the liberty to choose
her time, her place, her favor. The poet's buzz,
she finds, was prelude to a stinger, and she
the victim of its pregnant venom. Mired
in motherhood, her poet's fancy fired
(if fired at all) but muses not thus cumbered,
she drags her dreams through life like clanking chains."
He may be right regarding others, dear,
but with the fallen you can't be numbered.
Your gift for wonder and surprise sustains
you; your laughter alone belies the critic's sneer.

UNCLES

The uncle role is one
that fits the natural clown—
or hero—or bore. On Sundays
uncles sit around
talking and showing you how
not to be alive
or clatter and tease and shout
till their worryful wives
tell them to stop. When your dad
scolds you for some crime,
an uncle remembers how mad
Grampa was that time
your father frightened a horse
on purpose and caused it to bolt;
and you notice there's no remorse
mixed with their laughter. Droll
or drab, crabby or kind,
uncles belong, no doubt.
No one would recommend
trying to do without them.
But wayward uncles are best:
reckless, rackety rogues
with jokes and yarns and a taste
for gifts that pinch or explode.
They mean their tricks to amuse
and the scares they give aren't lasting,
for nothing an uncle can do
hurts like a father's blessing.

AUNTS

Aunts are not ashamed to talk about
what troubles them, as uncles are;
and even when their worry seems
excessive, their candor makes us care.

Does their candor or our concern
or both or neither account for their
longevity? They outlast uncles
mostly. Perhaps because they share

sorrows (whereas uncles hoard them)
they have a lighter load to bear?
But aunts seem never not busy:
even ensconced in easy chairs

chatting, they pry and their eyes wander
seeking what's to be done and where
is best to begin. But who has known
an aunt with no time to spare

for gossip, laughter, food and mourning?

ENOUGH'S ENOUGH

Hello? Is that you, Dorothy?
. . . You wondered what? . . . Oh, yes, we made it home
all right, but all the same I must have wished
a thousand times we'd stayed all night at your place.
. . . Yes, I know you asked us to, but you
know Mark! And then he'd had that brandy, too.
. . . Oh, no, I don't blame Melvin—at least, not much.
It's Mark should have known better, what
with the roads as slippery as they are . . . . The fog?
We had it all the way. The farther we went
the worse it got. We had the windows down
but even so I couldn't see a thing.
I have to give Mark credit: he did keep
from landing in a ditch. I might's well
tell you everything that happened. Mark
already made a yarn of it. He called
Jessies' this morning even before he did
the chores, and after breakfast he drove to town
so now I s'pose that half the countryside
has heard how clever he is. I'm glad you called:
at least I'll have the pleasure of telling *you*
before he does. It's something to steal his thunder.
. . . No, he didn't, Dorothy. He drove
as slow and careful as I could ever wish.
I know that doesn't sound like Mark, but—What?
. . . Well, this was worse than that time, even so.
We must have been a full half-hour on the road
when he began cussing worse than ever.
He said he'd missed a turn and we were lost.
I tell you, Dorothy, I was scared enough
to stop right there and wait for the fog to lift.

But Mark was in no mood for my suggestions
and anyway, my feet were cold and wet.
I'd stepped in a puddle in your driveway . . . . What?
. . . Yes, the heater works all right, but with
the windows down, what good's a heater do?
Anyway, at first we'd seen some lights
here and there along the road, and met
some cars, but by the time we lost our way
everyone with any sense was sleeping.
We started watching for a farmhouse
so we could stop and get directions. Well,
whenever I would say I saw one, Mark
would stop the car and look and tell me I need
new glasses . . . . No, I couldn't, Dorothy:
as soon as he would stop, whatever it was
I thought I saw would simply disappear.
At last he turned in at a farm *he* saw
and stopped beside a gloom that could have been
a house or barn or *any*thing. He said,
"Go and ask these people where we are."
. . . No, of course I didn't. He *knew* I wouldn't.
I told him he should be the one to ask.
He said, "Well, stay in the blanketty car then, dammit!"
He shut the engine off and slammed the door
and went. You know how fog muffles sound?
His knocking made a noise like—nothing else.
I rolled the windows up and started the engine
hoping I could get my shoes dried out.
After awhile a light went on downstairs
and then another upstairs. Dorothy,
you can't imagine how they made me feel,
those lights. I'd almost come to think
there was no one in the world but Mark and me

and the foolish frogs chirping in the ditches.
. . . No, *frogs*. I s'pose it's all these rains
have filled the ditches with them. Anyway,
I waited and waited and shivered and waited. I thought
that Mark must know the folks who lived there to spend
so much time talking. And then I wondered why
they didn't ask me in if they were friends
of ours. But it seemed likely Mark had just
forgot that I was there—you know him
when he begins to gab! I noticed that
the gas gauge was showing almost empty
so I shut the engine off. I don't know
how long I sat there waiting, but at last
I seemed to recognize the little shed
in front of me, and then the house began
to look familiar, too. And then it hit me:
we were home and Mark had gone to bed!
. . . Yes! . . . Well, I suppose it is funny,
but it *wasn't*, not last night. I went upstairs
and climbed in bed and lay there cold as a stone.
Mark pretended he was sound asleep
but pretty soon the bed began to shake
and then he broke out laughing. He'd still be laughing
if he hadn't got a coughing fit.
I had my revenge, though—he had to let
me warm my feet all night against his bottom!
. . . What? . . . Well, thanks for calling, Dorothy.
It's nice to know you cared enough to worry
even though it seems so funny now.
I'll try to laugh along with you when Mark
tells it with all the silly stuff he'll add.
Really, Dorothy! It isn't all that funny!
Now you'll go tell Melvin, I suppose.

After all these years with Mark, I should
be used to folks laughing like fools at me.
I don't have to stand here listening to
it, though. Enough's enough! Goodbye!

THE NECESSARY WORLD

I

Rolling sibilance of passing cars;
sleepy flutter of flames on the gas grate;
the sighs and tossings of his wife and daughters,
who dream apart, each in her own darkness—
these rhythms resist the clock's inane,
insistent reckoning. He shuts his eyes
to see the world alive and whole again.

II

How lovely they had been, sharing in
Pinnochio's pranks! The children snuggled to
their mother on the couch, clinging to
her bare arms and vivid voice. Soft rain
drifted down the dusky windows. Rapt
in puppet mischief that causes real distress,
the little girls were quiet then for once.

When the children had been put to bed, he helped
with the washing up, and learned how slyly she
had compromised the day's fractious demands.
He tried to give his own account a lilt
as merry. Then they sat before the fire,
she to brush her hair, he with a book,
though what he read was her loveliness.

But when she rose and asked if he was ready,
he shook his head reluctantly. "I think
I'll read awhile," he said, lifting up
the open book he had scarcely been aware
was in his lap. "I'm sleepy anyway,"
she said, and leaned to kiss his offered lips.
Her loose hair felt like rain against his cheek.

III

The gladness that had bloomed throughout the evening
withered in the desert her leaving made.
Thinking of familiar ways he failed
today and how such failings, shared by millions,
mount, become the monstrous tidings blared
on airwaves, he doubts the wisdom of
The Wisdom of the West, lays it aside.

Heraclitus . . . had he too been reared
beside a river, his mind modeled on
a cloudy, restless mirror? But rivers can't
run backward as his mind does now, recalling
pasture elms draped with wild grapevines;
cliffs that crumbled as he and his brother climbed them;
and quick as wonder a wilderness of creatures.

Once an oriole, like a lesser sun
setting over fields of fragrant snow,
alighted in a thicket of wild plum,
then flashed away never to return
except in memory. Was it that same
spring he lost his single-hearted faith
while lying fallow on a sun-mulled sandbar?

Lazy as he, the lurking fish declined
the barbed worms he offered. Riversounds
and sun beguiled him into a trance of doubt:
if everything must die at last, why live?
Gazing at the sun, he fell in dazzled
darkness, clenched his eyelids, fingers. Sand
and sense alike trickled from his grasp.

In time his mother called him. Judy-like
and apron-semaphoring she appeared
atop the cliff that overbrowed the river.
Scolding was her career. But he was glad
this once at having chores to do, and leaped up
waving and shouting like a stranded sailor
hailing a speck that may become a ship.

And all that summer after, he had know
as never before and seldom since how dear
life is. Uncles and cousins, at war across
and on the oceans, stopped playing hero
in his daydreams, lived the fear he felt
for them. His parents' quarrels angered him:
why did they waste their precious lives that way?

Then, angry at his anger, another waste,
he'd run to the river, fall on the sand, feel
his breath and blood rushing through him. As
they slowed, he'd feel the world again. Sometimes
he thought his heart would break if meadowlark
replied once more to meadowlark, or hawk
wheeled 'round heaven's axle one more time.

His heart, however, tougher than he thought,
had learned to bear the beauty it must lose.
More and more he lived beyond his means
of understanding, seeking what seemed good,
complaining of man's condition and of men,
but hoping somehow something, God's will
perhaps, would shine forth to show the way.

This new war in Asia—is it now
we blow the world to bits? If not this time,
the next. And someday the sun itself will die.
O for the grace to honor life as gift—
a present, the present, this moment.
The necessary world is now, and here
the lucky chance to serve, to choose and cherish.

IV

The candid clock tells him that now is *now,*
that he is here and chose to be here now
as husband, father, sneaking seeker, loser;
one of a multitude that slide along
on nature's bounty, their coffins on the backs
and sentient horns aquiver. Was it for them
that Titans troubled heaven and Jesus bled?

Ashamed, but leery of his shame, he yawns
and sees a mocking mask agape at him.
Another room—like his, a gleaming shadow—
dangles in the void outside his window.
To exorcise the ghost he snaps a switch
and stands in darkness, musing on the lights
that mark the city's hills like fallen stars.

Assured that some will keep the world for him
to wake to, as he has done for them at times,
he goes to check his daughters, and smiles to see
how buoyantly they sprawl in vivid postures.
He kneels to kiss them. Unaccustomed to prayer,
he holds its attitude until his knees
remind him he is still an infidel.

V

He strips in darkness and slides between the sheets.
Forgiving life for being too profuse
and makeshift for him to comprehend, he turns
to his sleeping wife as leaves turn to the sun.
And when his body's touch awakens her
whose beauty has awakened him tonight,
he quite forgets life ever needed pardon.

San Francisco, 1964

THE GIFT

I

Sunday afternoon I drove to the farm
and found Father in his recliner, dying.
"Can't seem to get my breath—too warm
in here." A shiver shook him as flying
leaves ticked on the window. "I went outside
this morning," he said. "Everything looks good,
don't it?" Praising this last crop of his
and the weather, I turned my head away as he tried
to fill his faltering lungs. Helpless, I stood
and stretched and walked about the room to ease
the cramp in my chest. "This is no day
for staying in. Go see if there's any chores
need doing." Perhaps he wanted me to stay
really, but I could draw a full breath outdoors.

II

My brother and I chose a burial plot
in the small rural cemetery that Father
had helped tend when he was a boy. On hot
days he and his three boisterous brothers
swam in the creek that curls at the base of the hill
where the graveyard sits. A greener age has passed
since they and their sisters imagined derring-do
to cram their days with: deeds and misdeeds to tell
over and over, making their childhood last
all their work-worn lives. The stories grew
more real with every telling, and more strange—
as strange and real as the straw-thatched shed
they burned with cattle in it, whose vivid revenge
was to always awfully die, yet never be dead.

III

After the prayers and preaching, after the songs,
the long ride: an hour of small talk
and large silences. No doubt we were wrong
not to admire the fields and herds and flocks
we passed; but without his praise, how could they please
us? A slow time, but too soon we were there,
and found a group of quiet farmers waiting.
Straight from their fields they had come, with dusty clothes
and faces, knowing he would approve such bare
obeisance to death. I had been near forgetting
how he would survive in men who had shared his life.
His way of being, having, doing,
informed those dusty farmers and their grief:
they had already forgiven him for dying.

IV

After potluck Sunday family dinners
we boys would pester our fathers into play—
ball or matches of strength and skill that the winners
as much as the losers winced to remember on Monday:
although inured to labor, their muscles rebelled
at the strange demands of festival. If Dad was vain
at all, it was his strength he gloried in.
Only exhaustion could make him yield.
He *would* hold the maul longer than anyone
straight out from his straining shoulder; chin
himself more times; do a "Cossack" dance
that sent his imitators tumbling. With what
delight he watched them sprawl! And when his stunts
were capped (rarely) his applause was, at best, polite.

V

He relished puns ("The worse the better," he said);
was hardly ever too busy to stop
and share a loaf of spicy stories; and had
in ready wit a never-failing crop.
Once he told me slyly, "You'll have to write
The Great American Novel, Dave, to make
an honest woman of your grandma." Our most
"religious" aunt, whose pleasure was to indict
her neighbors' pleasures, almost choked on her cake
when Dad proposed this anniversary toast:
"George Wood but Anna Wouldn't." My favorite, though,
was when he told a tight-fisted lout
who sneered a giving, "The saddest men I know
have money to burn after their fire's gone out."

VI

Ten years before he died he scraped together
at last a down-payment on a farm of his own:
weed-choked fields and sagging buildings. The weather
blessed his vision with crops better than he had grown
ever before. He rebuilt the dim,
despondent house and barn; and planted more
than a thousand trees, though they would grow too slow
to give much shade or shelter to Mother and him.
He grew some flax most years, for the flowers it bore—
sky's echo; and walked through his fields with a hoe
and scythe to make them tidy as a park.
Friends had tried to dissuade him from buying such
a ruin, but now admired his handiwork.
He'd grin: "Your praise don't tickle me—not much!"

VII

Knowing he'd made his last crop, he sold
at auction all the tools of his trade, stuff
that he had bought, mostly, when it was old
already by someone's standard. "It's hard enough
to make a go of farming," he believed;
"when a banker buys you new machinery, it only
helps you dig a deeper hole to fall in."
The auctioneer gabbled and Father grieved
as if old friends were being slandered. Lonely
amid the skeptical bidders, he watched them hauling
his livelihood away: tractors, plow,
combine, 'picker, planters, fencing, ropes,
shovels, feedbunks, wagons, rotary hoe—
the much-mended embodiment of used hopes.

VIII

Destined through most of his open-handed life
to practice in others' fields his farmer's craft;
tested by all the tangled demands of a wife
and children; winding up on the cruel shaft
cancer—he never let fortune bully him:
it took death to dam his quiet flow
of gaiety and goodness. Even now
those shining waters tremble on the brim,
and now they tumble over to bestow
their benison again: remembering how
his hands and heart made fields and friendship thrive,
remembering *him*, I give my grief short-shrift.
When he so gladly gave himself to life,
how can I but gladly keep the gift?

TO MY BROTHER

(Inscribed in a gift of the Tao-te-Ching)

The Tao is where one finds it—
    when one is not looking
    mostly.

It overflows with surprises
    that always fit their occasions
    neatly.

The Tao has no words
    but is as fluent as water or
    feeling;

like a rambling stream, it chuckles
    chidingly at pointless
    strivings.

So why do I seek words
    to tell you how the Tao
    happens?

—*You* with whom the Tao
    seems friendly as a playful
    puppy.

SISTERS

(As Seen by Younger Brothers)

Sisters tattle, then regret
the fury they have loosed.
In fights they are reduced to screams
and fingernails and shoes.

In later life, their grace surprises you.

A NOTHING GIFT

There's nothing that a man can give
to her who has his all already—
unless he slyly steal his love
from her, mend such holes as steady
use will wear in any weave,
then pledge his all again. But could he,
in the leaden meanwhile, live
uncommitted to his lady?
Or what if she, relieved, should thrive
without his love, and spurn it gladly?

Rather than try such perilous theft
I offer you this nothing gift.

IN PRAISE

I

It's true those birds are strutting when they sing,
Not praising you; the stately August sun
Parades its pomp to please itself alone,
Regardless of your pleasure; these roses fling
A fragrance on the air and children run
In leaping loops across our ragged lawn
Simply to celebrate their self-content.
Exactly so I have conceived these poems
Only to give exulting ego vent;
For I proclaim my luck by praising you,
And commandeer your beauty for my theme
Less to honor than to lean on it.
If I had skill enough, however, to
Create your image here—that would redeem
Even my parasitical conceit.

II

On your knees, among your flowers; hair
catching sunlight to fabricate a crown;
competent hands (how beautiful with dirt!)
waving away a pertinacious blur
of midges; freckled brow knit in a frown
of down-in-earth thought—you are alert
to intercept the garden's diligent foes:
slugs and bugs and weeds and other woes—
all but winter's advent. From the first
green push of spring to the first fell frost
you lend a critical hand to nature, yet never
rebel at the ravage of colors you have nursed.
Are you content because, though blooms may be lost,
honest pensees last almost forever?

III

Chin on hand, you work a problem out;
and though I watch its pressures mold your brow,
you occupy a realm remote from me:
mathematics. Wont to muck about
and somehow muddle through, I envy now
and then the neat, provisional certainty
you know in that spooky universe,
which may or may not, for better or worse,
last longer than this untidy world we share.
But mostly I rejoice to have you go
alone there—your eyes keen where mine are dim—
and bring back eerie stones for me to stare
at: love, like friendship, prospers on the flow
from private fountains flooding over the brim.

IV

Though other women too have clever talk
that wins my ear and sets my tongue to prancing,
only you have silences that sing.
To share an open fire with you; to walk
with you in winter streets, the snowflakes dancing
'round anchored moons; to wake early on spring
mornings and find in you as in the year
renewal—such stillness tunes our spirits, dear.
But talk we must of what the children need
and how to guide them; of housework; plumbing, bills,
and all the toils of love: homely themes
that exercise our wits and so provide
earnest play for our contending wills.
How deftly love accommodates extremes!

V

For luxury I recall the twists you surprise
the children with when you embroider an hour
with homespun yarns; the messages you plant
in unexpected places; your clownish guise
when, kneading bread, you smudge your cheek with flour;
our genial disagreements; the way you slant
a truth so children can climb it; your sly defenses
against prying; your nudging, sidewise glances;
the tasks you vent exasperation through;
the way your candor derails a train of clichés;
the warm perfume and taste and soft touch
you are. Choosing to share restraints with you
has tethered me in clover most days
and nights. What other bond could yield so much?

VI

When some other lovely woman charms my eye,
arousing drowsy lust, if I invoke
the image of your beauty to displace
the call of hers, you bloom like breaking day
across my mind, bearing the ancient yoke
of motherhood and marriage with such grace
the other's charm fades like a laggard moon
overtaken by the enterprising sun.
But consider how the moon bewitches sight:
appearing now as amber, now as snow,
now quick and slender, now full and ripe and slow;
while like the summer sun you lend your light
so lavishly I take it as my due,
am grateful least when most in debt to you.

VII

Deferring to your candor, I won't pretend
your virtues and your beauty never lose
their brightness for me: sometimes I cultivate
a grouch until it shades all sense; or lend
myself to fame-and-fortune fantasies;
or, mocking honest conscience, calculate
my worth in troubles earned and chances lost.
At such times I perceive you through the mist
that veils my vain abstraction: when you speak,
I only hear a dim, familiar noise;
and when you touch, you hand is but a hand.
Then sudden as waking, welcome as spring, you break
sun-like through the fog: again the blaze
your beauty makes relumes my heart and mind.

VIII

The afternoon we first made love together—
through happy chance we had your brother's flat
just to ourselves, remember? And how the world
fell darkly into a spell of heavy weather?
An April snowstorm! But we were too elate
to heed winter's return, and freely unfurled
our leaves and petals. After, still abloom
with pleasure, I capered to my distant room
through drifts I would have plodded through before;
having shared with you that tonic fever
I thought the whole world must someday warm
to love's genial motive. But lies, war,
injustice blast as many lives as ever.
The world still stumbles blindly from storm to storm.

IX

Was it authentic vision or mere delusion,
that Someday world at home with love? Could we
be happy there? Or does our happiness
require this sense of sense amid confusion,
of luck among a luckless throng? To be
implicated in the world's distress
but not disheartened by it argues, perhaps,
complacency: a paralyzed synapse
between the world and conscience. Then what moves
us to reach out and try to find our neighbor
everywhere, and most in foul weather?
Responsibility begins in love's
delight and grows with love itself in labor:
like roots and crown they ramify together.

TO MOTHER

I've stayed home from work today to nurse a cold.
Outside the window pop-art crystal carrots
hang from the eaves. Sparrows bounce and bicker
among the lilac's bare branches. Maybe they quarrel
to warm themselves?

Alice at work and the girls in school. The furnace makes
a long-winded companion, stopping now and then to catch
its breath or maybe to let me get a word in edgewise
if I've a mind to. Luckily I don't, for if I did
the furnace wouldn't listen anyway.

The house is a warm, brooding womb with a view. Almost
I wish not to recover soon from this "cold" inside myself
To tangle with that truer cold outside the house.
O these nine-months-long Minnesota winters!

When summer comes at last, will I remember to recall
how well the house has sheltered me? I doubt it.
But houses learn with mothers how to care:
they take us as we are and as we need them.

ANOTHER FOR MOTHER

I can never be grateful enough
for the generous gift of life:
for the months you carried me,
a true skin-diver
in the Amniotic Sea;
for the hours of pulsing labor
that pushed me into the air;
for all the work that followed.
(I wonder: how could you bear
my messes? You that are hurt
by mere natural clutter
and agonized by dirt!)

For years you spoiled the rod
and scared the child, breathing
the wrath of a living Goddess,
your storms sudden, blinding,
unappeasable. In time
your lightning fizzled, and finding
you uncertain, I turned
away to live as I would.
But as I lived I learned
simple gratitude
(though surely never enough)
for the chancy charmer, life.

TO OUR CHILDREN

We conceived you without thought
simply in our delight.
Unlooked-for dividends,
you've kept our hearts and minds
engaged ever since.
Creative consequence
indeed, for thus we owe
as much being to you
as you to us. Now, if
we honor this fact of life—
this mutual, vital debt—
we more than merely accept
its claims: we celebrate
the harvest of delight,
responsibility.
When one and one make three
or more, that's loves own
but not its only boon.

PARABLE OF
THE BRANCHES

Its blossoms stripped,
the cherry bough springs back,
a vengeful whip.

The girl who tore its flesh
goes off singing
and never feels the lash.

Not so the bough's companions:
shivering at the sudden blow
they drop their snow.

TO AN ANGRY DAUGHTER

I've thought about your anger long tonight
until at last its fiery core
kindles remorse. (Or was my heartburn lit
merely by too much coffee?) Anyway,
I feel the justice of your indignation:
why should one whose chief accomplishment
has been to father three promising children
ask them to use their lives and talents well?
It's true I hope to see the light that's in you
compensate for all the fuel I've wasted
burning bridges behind me, and I would bask
in your achievements as if they were my own.
However selfish my motives are, ignore them.
You must answer for your gifts someday
(some night, more likely) not to me, but to
the soul you're making every time you choose.

TO DARE TO BE

Our nature sets this subtle snare
for those who lead a seminar—
for parents, too:
we learn by doing what we dare
but teach by being what we are.

THE DURABLE OLD

The young can think of nothing more depressing
than being lectured by the durable old,
especially when they hear the old confessing,
"When I was young I never would be told,
refused my elders' words, likewise their blessing,
and learned the hard way that tinsel isn't gold.
Good God! The rainbows I went chasing
when I was young! I never would be told!"

What saddens sophomores when they hear such talk
is not the fear they too will make mistakes.
They sense already that Pegasus may balk,
that things in which they trust will turn out fakes.
No, this is why they listen leaden-eyed:
the old remember failure with such pride!

THE FAMILY OF MAN

I

God respected Abel's bloody gift
but spurned the fruits of tillage Cain tendered.
Cain was wroth, and who can wonder why?
If God favored blood, then Cain would spill it.
God, it seemed, was still dissatisfied.
The lesson? Who can say? The Bible doesn't.
Maybe God intended to convey
that only they can please Him whom He chooses
(Calvin read the story so). Perhaps
He meant to show that we should stick to what
we know and love, regardless of reward.
Or maybe He intended nothing (*that*
would be the hardest lesson He could set).

II

I've been looking over yet again
"the greatest photographic exhibition
of all time," which Edward Steichen made
"to demonstrate the oneness of mankind
throughout the world." Not so artful as God,
Steichen lays his lesson on the line.
I don't want to quarrel with the goal
of world-wide amity, but BROTHERHOOD
may be the worst of slogans. Those first brothers
left us lasting food for thought. Though we
may be repelled by its ambiguous smell
and bitter flavor, dare we decline the fare?

III

Devoted sons, my uncles Mark and Bill
turned their backs on Grandma's last request:
to shake hands across her deathbed, lay
to rest the quarrel they had nursed so long
that none but them (if they) recalled its birth.
Years later, as Mark himself lay dying
slowly agonized by awful burns,
he told me how and why he so disliked
the doctor who was keeping him alive
against his will: "He can't believe that I
might know what's best for me; he's just like Bill."

IV

One night when I was twelve I entertained
my brother by going mad: with rolling eyes,
a racking twitch, drooling and gibberish mixed
with threats, I had him laughing for awhile.
But then he turned thoughtful and told me to quit.
I grabbed a butcher knife: "I'ze gwine t'cut
yo gizzuhd out!" Don didn't know the line
from *Penrod*, ran screaming, thrusting chairs
between us. And after him I came so near
to genuine madness I shiver remembering it.

V

But why assert the lurking ghost of Cain?
I live in a city famed for healing, a fame
founded on the work of brothers. Will
and Charlie Mayo, suckled on the wolf
Disease, grew wise and rich and old together.
They shared such wisdom as their town would take

from them, and much of their wealth. This city thrives
by striving to redeem the body's health
as Rome once throve on hopes of the soul's redemption.

VI

It was the Mayos' reaching out to serve
the afflicted family of man that brought
them close enough together to heal fraternal
rivalry. Will was "trim, incisive,
reserved." Charlie "looked like a grocer," "became
at once the friend of everyone he met."
Each found his own identity in the vast
community of human suffering.

VII

For humankind to celebrate a new
millennium, we must engage our troubles.
We come to grief by trying to go around
it now: pursuing happiness we stumble
into envy, boredom. Happiness
is what happens to us while we do
our best; is seldom recognized till past.

VIII

In Steichen's book, however, happiness
and grief are less than likeness is: this clan
of Kalahari Bushmen could stand in
for folks I gossip with at family picnics.
But how can I endure my mother's woes?
And why are my own children sometimes strangers?

IX

Until I comprehend my nearest kin,
respect their troubles and accept their sins,
what good can come of loving as I do
this naked, withered Bushman who delights
his desert clan with sprightly click-tongued tales?

X

Love, the true charity, begins
at home for most of us; survives at home
only if it sends out roots and branches
into every life that it can reach.

XI

Maybe Cain would not have been so wroth
to see his brother favored if the lives
of both had been enlarged by friending others.

XII·

Soon enough we go, each one of us
alone, to death's dark wilderness—

XIII

but here can practice love's eternal now.

A TRUE VOCATION

"What do you want to do when you grow up?"

I couldn't decide except that I knew quite young
I didn't want to farm (we milked cows
twice a day, seven days a week—
a form of slavery). I went to college
hoping to find the answer there, and found
a heap of things I liked. But nothing grabbed
me, saying, "This is what you're meant to do."
Over the next thirty years I worked
as a psychiatric tech while in the Army,
as a truck dispatcher, as an advertising
copywriter (YUCK!). I taught school
for ten years and loved it, but—sadly—lacked
the energy to do it all my life.
I wrote or edited Proceedings, abstracts,
indices and other entertaining
stuff for the Mayo Clinic Section of
Neurology. I counseled veterans and job
seekers and job losers and job avoiders
for the macho State of Minnesota.
(What other state has chosen a governor
to *wrestle* with its problems?) In the cracks
between these jobs I've been a carpenter,
factory worker, gardener, sometimes a poet.
All but one of these occupations blessed
me in some way. (The one I hated might
someday have made my fortune, but whatthehell!)
None was what I wanted to do when I
grew up, so I just never quite grew up.

Till I became a grandfather. Yes,
a GRANDFATHER! This is what I want
to do! O Kira, Ellen, David, Ruby,
Jack, Olivia, Sam, Alice and Andre!
You're my calling, my profession, my
career. For you I have at last grown up
to second childhood, where being, doing, playing
once again outrank mere getting and having.

TO ROBERT BURNS

My great-grandmother Burns,
whose boldest oaths were *darns,*
was pleased to claim you as her husband's kin.
She alleged direct descent
and I am confident
the claim was relatively genuine:
though she might sometimes hide
the truth, she rarely lied
outright, except as a social discipline.

Though vices in her neighbor
and family dismayed her,
she found some saving grace in all *your* sins;
and that's as well, I think,
for maybe my first link
with you (if any) was one of your bastart weans.
But you will not disown me
for that, Rab, if only
your gift for loving live yet in my genes.

(I hope that you forbear
my puns, at least.) Heir
or not, I gladly cherish your generous spirit.
Your colorful Scottish speech,
unfaded by the bleach
that grizzles heads, is hale as vintage claret.
Like Chaucer you can give
delight enough to live
"till all the seas gang dry," or very near it.

To you that salty phrase
meant *forever;* nowadays
it sounds like dire though commonplace prediction:
as lakes and rivers die
and the Aral Sea goes dry,
we moderns may be the planet's last affliction,
committing ecocide
as we attempt to hide
our nakedness with leaves from science fiction.

You'll note I speak as if
we cling to an icy cliff
that formerly was fertile, level land.
This tremulous conceit
may puzzle you, whose feet
swung over voids as dark to comprehend
as those we fear. Still,
our troubles do compel
us uniquely: now the whole of humankind

depends on a single rope:
respect for life. To grope
and grab and fumblefoot for holds to enhance
one's state is ruinous when
scrambling can only strain
the fraying strands. It won't be mere mischance
if the rope breaks: we know
our peril, but act as though
our interest lies in polished ignorance.

Not that we are worse
than the characters your verse
is peopled with. They'd gape awhile at our
invented world, no doubt—
amazed that we dare flout
so brazenly the lesson of the Tower
of Babel. But they would see
(when wonder passed) that we
but bring their frauds and follies into flower.

Our Tam O'Shanters have
no sober Meg to save
the day. Now when a drunkard heads for home
there are more than a hundred horses
bearing him—perforce as
drunk as he. Caparisoned in chrome
and bright enamel, these
unfeeling, spurious steeds
run thousands yearly down the track of doom.

Expecting that God *earn*
their approbation, modern
Holy Willys seldom kneel to pray
for favors, but they still
identify God's will
as what they want to do—that is to say,
they have a right to what
they want and others not
so blessed had better yield. As in your day

authorities conspire
to bank erotic fire
lest all that energy be spent before
youngsters can be caught
in coils of duty: taught
to serve and honor industry and war
the benefits of which,
as ever, bathe the rich
while the scummy overflow bemires the poor.

Speaking of industry,
yours amazes me:
so great a volume of accomplishment
in so abridged a life!
I wonder: did your wife
provide much of the fund of wit you spent
as yours? (But having picked
wedlock, who keeps strict
account of borrowings?) As the monument

at Alloway rose, your Jean
brandished a claymore keen:
"He asked for bread and they're giving him a stane!"
Rab, you must admit
your satire seldom hit
its targets neater. Mockery is vain,
though: frauds and bigots flourish
yet, and poets nourish
song with vitals (their families' as their own)

or song would surely starve.
Besides, it takes a nerve
like yours and mine to blame bad faith. Just think
how you once made a plan
to drive your fellow man
in slave Jamaica—you that lavished ink
on praise of brotherhood!
That ill-laid scheme (thank good-
ness!) went agley, thus saving you for drink,

disease, poverty,
labor and poetry.
The burdens that wore you out are a mute refrain
that shadows all you wrote,
deepening your gladdest note.
Only by sweating under a load of pain
and loss and error can Yea-
saying love and joy
be earned on Earth. Your right to them is plain,

and though one can't inherit
goods that each must merit
or miss, when I breathe the bonny airs you left
to me, to every man,
my grateful lungs expand
exultantly.
Did you resign your craft
at last, or do you now
sing behind The Plow
where no mouse shivers in the coulter's cleft?

PART TWO

Vivid Ghosts

VIVID GHOSTS

The days stretched out before us like
a desert, and we yearned toward our
deliverance (our discharge dates)
as children yearn toward Christmas. Cast
like dice in Yahtzee, we found ourselves
among a strange array of strangers:
one who couldn't read and one
with a master's in philosophy;
one Australian who would not
become a U.S. citizen
till he completed his two years
of service; some worldly; some
naïve; some gentle by nature or
by nurture (some by both, perhaps)
and some as tough as life could make
them. Even the conscientious objectors
were near as varied as the mass
of humankind. In medical basic
training I knew one who found
the Army so congenial to
his taste for order he applied
for OCS and was accepted,
shucking off his fundamentalist
faith like an ill-fitting suit.

A few were married and lived off-base
with their wives, but most of us had to live
in barracks: cot, footlocker,
locker, with two feet of space
between the cots. Propinquity
made friends or foes of men who would

have had no feelings for each other
if there had been a living space
between their egos. My best friend
was Bill Bryant, as unlike me
as anyone I've known. He loved
to hunt and fish, and while I've done
a bit of both, they never won
my heart. He seldom read a book,
but argued well about the ones
he did read. He delighted in fighting
while I had always turned away
from conflict. Somehow we contrived
to let our differences produce
the changes in ourselves that made
our friendship flourish. We exchanged
a flurry of letters in our first
year of freedom, and he came
to visit us in California
once. But that was long ago
and where he's gone or how he's done
I'll never know. The only one
of all those comrades I still see
from time to time I see because
his sister married me. The others
and the patients we attended
have become vivid ghosts,
rising greenly into lives
that they abandoned long ago.

CRABS BACKLASH

As if to lop off any budding hubris,
this medical basic training company
is nibbled by pediculosis pubis
and suffers a humbling, biting agony
of itching while standing at distracted attention.
Even those who doubt that they are hosts
feel bitten now, stretched to full tension
on racks in ranks while the chaplain roasts
them in his wholly rhetorical fire. They squirm
as much as they are able, waiting for
dismissal. Marched then into barracks, stripped
and dusted with DDT, they dare affirm
that they will never darken the chapel door
and, when in town, they'll keep their pants unzipped.

ANOTHER CHANCE

In college I was cast as Eilert Lovborg
in Hedda Gabler, a role I might have played
with credit a few years later—after
waking in a padded isolation room
on a locked psychiatric ward
where I was a psychiatric tech.
I had a broken jaw and hammering hangover.
I knew where I was but not how I had come there.

Friends had covered the observation window,
but I could hear the patients just outside
shuffling in their cloth slippers, giggling,
jostling one another for position,
hoping to tease me when the door was opened.
At last a tech and nurse came to see
if I was ready to rejoin the world.
It seemed the world would have me back
despite my glass jaw and shameful conduct.

Eilert should have got another chance,
but Ibsen couldn't end the play that way.

HIPSTER

A hip young man from Chicago, he riffed
on jazz as long as anyone
would listen (sometimes for himself
alone) imitating with
his lips and tongue and voice the sounds
he loved. He hadn't learned to play
an instrument: he couldn't choose
which one to give his loyalty to.
There was a cheap monophonic
record player on the ward,
and sometimes records, too. (The
hip young man insulted others freely;
they paid him back by smashing his
most prized possessions, records.) When Bird
warbled, squawked and trilled from tinny
speakers, the jazz enthusiast
would dance and scat and snap his fingers,
shuffling in his cloth ward slippers,
blue pajamas flapping. He
was cool as anyone could be
without a potent hair-straightener
and well-cut street-smart clothes, lacks
he frequently complained about.
He was one of several patients
who seemed quite as sane as we
technicians felt ourselves to be,
but wearing the tag "psychotic" he
indulged his moods more freely than
we dared. Though not an easy man
to get along with, he could make
the ward throb with liveliness.

INCIDENT IN A BARRACKS

He worked the night shift on a ward
of wounded soldiers (many also
suffering from TB before
there was effective treatment for it)
and went to the hospital mess alone
for breakfast. We remembered later
seeing him there, hunched above
his tray, morosely poking food
into his mouth. He seemed to have
no friends. Even other sergeants
passed him by to join groups
of bantering laughers. After breakfast
he went to his stark room at the head
of a barracks stairway, for a change
not badgering the privates who
had bunks in the common rooms. He may
have slept for awhile or may have started
drinking right away. By 6
PM when the loudspeaker on
the watertower began to blare
a scratchy recording of Retreat
(an everyday occurrence) he
was thoroughly soused. Against the rules
he had live ammunition in
his room, and used it in his carbine
to shoot the loudspeaker from
his window. Soon a frightened squad
of MPs appeared with bull-
horns, asking everyone
to clear the area. Few did, of course:

we thought we knew which window he
had fired from, kept as clear of that
as we could, but stayed nearer than
was wise so we could monitor
the situation. Bullhorns blared
demands: PUT THAT RIFLE DOWN
AND COME DOWNSTAIRS. DO IT NOW!
There may have been some threats, too.
After several minutes he
appeared at the foot of the stairs, swaying,
holding a pistol in each hand.
A psychiatrist we knew came then,
and bravely entered the barracks to talk
with him in a gentle, calming voice.
We couldn't hear their brief exchange,
but felt relieved to see the sergeant
seem to waver, listen, wait
for enlightenment, a way to decide.
Then suddenly he raised the pistols
to his head and ended his
involvement in this life
that caused him too much pain. Even
the men he'd harshly supervised
and who had thought they hated him
found reasons to admire him now.

FOXY MOLE

He killed a man in a riot
in the Disciplinary Barracks at
Fort Benning, Georgia; then,
while serving a life sentence at
Fort Leavenworth, he killed a guard
who was, he said, turning him
into a mole. "Just look at all
this fur all over me!" And truly
he had more hair than most men
on powerful arms and shoulders, chest
and back and legs, and Brylcremed
just-so black waves on his head,
and a thin Errol Flynn moustache
he trimmed fastidiously each day
with a razor we unlocked for him.
His tale about becoming a mole
persuaded some psychiatrists
that he was crazy. "Crazy like
a fox," he sometimes slyly told
us psychiatric techs. Though seeking
always to dominate and keep
his fellows cowed, he was mostly cheerful
and knew how far his violence
could be let run on the locked-ward leash.
He conned a paperback about
the Mafia till it fell apart
despite all the Scotchtape
he begged from the nurses' station.
He had it memorized by that
time though, and freely quoted chapter

and verse to anyone who'd listen.
He aspired to be recruited by
The Mob, which "had its tentacles
in the White House" (a claim
that we were fools enough to doubt).
The gentle Quaker techs confessed
that though they trusted he had "that
of God" in him, they didn't trust
him. Before my own two years
had ended, he was transferred, sedated,
to a Veterans Hospital in Texas.
Drowsily but merrily
he swore that he'd be out of there
before we dumb, unlucky saps
had worked our way to freedom. We thought
it likely he could pull it off.

INSULIN SHOCK

A strapping farm kid, whose chest
and shoulders bulged from tossing bales
and similar chores, he didn't like
the Army, saw no sense in most
of what he was expected to do.
He was the kind of man who shows
affection and dislike alike
with punches—hard ones for those
who stirred his anger. That was why
he found himself (or so we guessed)
on a locked psychiatric ward.
So far as we could tell (and we
saw more of him than doctors did)
he was as sane as anyone
who called him crazy. He had been
with us for several months before
they started him on insulin shock.

About twenty patients came
to the treatment room each morning,
and climbed into beds in two long rows.
Nurses moved from bed to bed
to inject protesting patients with
a massive dose of insulin—
enough to put them into comas.
Several of us techs were there
to monitor and chart the pulse,
respiration, temperature
and blood pressure of each patient.
The doctor in charge strolled about,

attentive but inclined to joke
and flirt with nurses when he wasn't
checking reflexes or reading charts.
I don't know how he decided when
to pull them back, but one by one
he signaled us to start IVs
of glucose. When revived enough,
each patient was required to drink
a glass of orange juice laced
with glucose. Then they went to breakfast.

All the patients gained weight
on this regime, the strapping farm
kid more than most: from muscle man
to blimp. He hated it, and had
to be restrained before a nurse
could get the insulin into him.
His veins began to disappear
in flab, were hard to find with needles.
At last the day came when no one,
tech nor nurse nor doctor, found
a vein in either arm to start
the glucose. Finally, sweating and cursing,
the doctor got one going in
his groin but glucose this time failed
to raise the kid to consciousness.
His temperature began to rise
alarmingly. We packed him in ice,
and flinched to see the doctor shoving
ice cubes up his ass. He stayed
near death for thirty hours or more,
then slowly returned to our world,

but changed: not quite a vegetable
but unresponsive, quiet, wanting
to spend his time apart, alone.
After a month or so, they shipped
him out to a VA Hospital.

Insulin shock went out of fashion
not much later: no one improved
on it; some died; and one, at least,
lost his life, but kept on somehow.

BLACK BEAUTY

One of the few men I've known
for whom *beautiful* seemed more
appropriate than *handsome*, he
was blacker than any black I'd seen
till then. He looked like Nefertiti,
his nose as straight and finely flared,
his brow as noble. Broad-shouldered,
slim-hipped, his buttocks high
and prominent, he looked as smart
in ward pajamas as most men
look in well-tailored suits.
He moved with fluid grace, and sometimes
shadowboxed with such finesse
that no one dared to mess with him.
He never picked a fight or took
offense at trifles as his fellow
patients all too often did.
Suspicious, solitary, he
would stand apart observing life
as suffered there or stare out
a barred window, though there was not
much to look at in the yard.
He seldom talked to anyone,
and quite surprised me once: "You look
like Abe Lincoln!" Even so,
he seemed not to like or trust me:
like Lincoln, I was white and free.

A HARD LIFE

In 1940, at the age
of ten, he entered one of the Polish
concentration camps, a hard
school that failed to prepare him for
his hard life. His native tongues
were Polish and Yiddish. In the camp
he added German, French and Russian.
When the Russians overran
the camp, he fled with friends to the West
and lived in Displaced Person camps
till 1951, when he
at last was let to emigrate
to America. His sponsor was
a church in Chicago, where he soon
found work in a slaughterhouse, not
an occupation one would choose
to ease the troubled mind of a person
reared with violence. Perhaps
that's why his psychiatrist believed
his breakdown had begun before
the Army got a hold of him.
Though we technicians could conceive
that the pre-induction physical
had failed its purpose, we recalled
our early days in uniform
and wondered whether he had flashed
back to his early camp experience
when trapped again in senseless order.
But most of what we knew about
him came from his psychiatrist,

for he was mostly silent on
the ward. He talked to himself sometimes,
but not in English. When I saw
him last, he still was isolated
from his fellows, an island lapped
by the paranoia of other patients
and his own aura of fear.

DOCTOR PRIVATE SACKLER

With several years of practice to
his credit, also publications
in psychiatric journals, he
refused a commission, came to work
a private like ourselves. The chief
psychiatrist (a colonel) told
us we should treat him with the same
respect we gave to other doctors.
Was he kidding? Empty honor?
He was, of course, our hero and
we honored him like a dear friend
who's risen in the world but knows
he's human. The Service company
commander, Major Bates (or Master
Bates as we called him) set out
to make him rue his having quaintly
chosen conscience. But how can you
humiliate a dignified
but humble man? The major gave
the petty effort up, at last,
and treated him like all the rest
of us enlisted men. That
was all he wanted. On the ward
he earned our admiration and
our prompt attention to his needs,
expressed with friendly courtesy.
He was no intimate, did not
tell jokes and shoot the breeze with us
as some of the doctors did. When he
declined to be promoted to

the rank of corporal, Major Bates,
offended by the snub, again
made life as hard as he could for him.
When Dr. Sackler came on duty
next, we didn't applaud him only
because we feared embarrassing him.
No, it was more than that: some
of us had grabbed the bait and
now outranked our hero, whose consistent
sense of honor somehow shamed us.

IN SOLITARY

One of the prisoner-patients, he
was said to be paranoid
and prone to violence, but had
a locked room to himself not
because of that but because he had
a virulent form of tuberculosis.
We techs were told always to wear
a surgical mask when dealing with him
and to wash our hands with special care
when we were done. We autoclaved
his tableware and tray and dishes
when he was done with them, and cleared
the shower room before he bathed.
Other patients sometimes tried
to muscle in to satisfy
their curiosity or perhaps
to ease his awful isolation.
He had a toilet stool in his room,
but sometimes smeared his feces on
the little observation window.
We wondered if he wanted privacy
or attention? Lookers-in could see
what he was doing; he could see
near-nothing of the ward. It was,
effectively, but solitary
confinement, worse than the segregation
he'd known since childhood. Soon I stopped
wearing a mask when delivering
his meals, and tried hard to engage
him in conversation. He at first

seemed leery of attention, but
in time he started telling his
complaints (all justified, I thought)
and sometimes something of his life.
(I learned how lucky mine had been.)
He never threw a fit when I
was with him, as he sometimes did
with others. And I never tested
positive for TB—
maybe more of my dumb-luck.

ALL PASSION SPENT

Here's the story we were told:
He had a cushy job in Paris
driving a general 'round the city,
and had enough time off to court
a mademoiselle. One evening he saw
her dining with another man
at a sidewalk café. Consumed
by jealousy, his anger mounting
to rage, he dropped the general at
his destination and returned
to find them still engaged in what
he saw as amorous dalliance
(it turned out that the other man
was her brother). He stopped his jeep in traffic.
Dodging cars while pulling his pistol
from its holster, he ran across
the street and shot them dead, the girl
and her brother, raised the pistol to
his own head and managed to
perform what doctors called "as clean
and surgical a prefrontal
lobotomy" as they had seen.
When he recovered from the wound,
his wits but not his will survived.
On the psychiatric ward, he proved
clever at chess and checkers, and
was good enough at bridge to be
sought out as partner, though
he didn't care if he won or lost.
He could recall nothing of

the day that changed his life forever,
but understood when told what he
had done. He did recall the girl,
supposed that she had been "pretty,"
that maybe he had been "in love"
with her, though now he didn't feel
that she or anything had value.
He didn't care what happened to
his own diminished life or feel
regret for it or for the girl
or her brother. French courts refused
to try him, and the US Army
still didn't know what it should do
with him at the time that I
returned to civilian life, so how
they dealt with him I never learned.

To feel such passion once, but then
feel nothing! Nothing. Nothing.

ELECTROENCEPHALOGRAM

This curious machine, they say,
records the brain's activity.
The switch is on, the currents hum,
the subject looks a little glum,
the paper moves, the styli scratch
describing what's beneath his thatch.

He wonders if the pens can tell
his dreams of bliss, his dread of Hell.
(Although he knows Hell doesn't exist,
the ancient bugaboo persists
in troubling him, maybe because
his character is full of flaws.)

The priestess serving the machine—
hunched before it, starched and clean—
looks dull, a thought that comforts him
though why it should is rather dim.
Perhaps he wants her not to see
the heart of his brain's mystery.

Relaxed, his mind begins to wander.
Slouching here and climbing yonder
it lies at last in fields of roses.
See how pleasantly he dozes,
unaware of inky wiggles
simulating ghostly giggles.

OLD FRIENDS

I haven't seen him in more than thirty years
except in memory, where he appears
often. Most commonly he sits
before a chessboard, contemplating. It's
not easy to contemplate while three small sons
are using you for a jungle gym: one's
straddling his neck tugging at his hair;
another dances on his lap (I fear
for the poor man's manhood) trying to displace
the one on top; the third, with jam on his face,
is clinging to a pantsleg shouting, "Horsey!
Horsey!" Calmly plucking Ben from his neck,
Walt deposits him an arm's length away
and holds him there while moving a knight. Of course, he
now has Josh on his shoulders, but I'm in check
and ready to move rashly. A rare day
or night it was that I beat Walt at chess!
Nor could I match him other ways unless
I count my fascination watching him
watch termites eat his house. He honored them
for their insatiable, brooding industry.
He took his own work, teaching, as seriously
as they took tunneling in wood, and gave
his free hour freely all one term to save
(we hoped) a non-reading teenage kid
from his inaptitude. Nothing Walt did—
not phonics drills, tachistoscope, nor any
other tricks we knew then—helped the lad
distinguish *cat* from *canary*. No complaint
I heard from Walt, however, about the many

hours he lost in a fruitless cause. He had
the patience of an ever-tested saint,
which drove his waspish Betty up the wall.
And now I see them together: Betty small
even when six-months pregnant, hair in a neat
chignon, blue eyes flashing, spends her wit
on everything but most on grinning Walt,
who venerates the inexhaustible vault
she has to draw on.
That is how I want
to see them, how they mostly, dearly haunt
my memory, not as they truly were:
a mismatched couple mannerly at war.

PART THREE

Falling

GRAND CANYON

On one of our transcontinental
trips, we stopped at the South Rim
of the Grand Canyon, expecting *not*
to be impressed, but ever after
dreamed of going back. The year
I was to turn sixty-five,
we read an ad about a trip
that Wilderness Inquiry planned:
fifteen days of rafting down
the Colorado River, starting
at Lees Ferry and coming out
at Diamond Creek, putting in
September 17th and taking
out October 2nd. My birthday is
September 21st, and I
then thought I wanted not to reach
the age of doddering. Now who
could want a grander way to go
than falling off a cliff or drowning
in a Colorado River rapids?
September, with its cooler days,
appealed to us, for Alice steams
when there is more than temperate heat.
We couldn't think of any reason
not to take the trip, so paid
for it a full six months before
our putting in.

Only the Paul
Winter Consort captures with art

some of the Canyon's eerie splendor.
(They made the music there.) On the South
Rim that first time, we saw
what we supposed was a hawk or eagle
soaring down below us; then
we realized it was a plane!
The sheer magnificence of scale,
which dwarfs all else (oneself especially)
puts everything one thinks about
in proper scale. Fantastic forms
and colors, indescribable
and infinitely varied, stir
one to gratitude. If anyone
can witness all that grandeur and not
be moved to prayer—or something like it—
that person lacks capacity
for wonder, maybe for being fully
human (nobody knows the trouble
he's seen, the trouble he may inflict
on others). The River from the Rim
appears to be a country creek,
but riding on its rapid current one
cannot believe that all of it
gets used before it reaches the Gulf
of California. Riding that
unbridled rocky-muscled steed
one sees and hears and *feels* the Canyon
at its Grandest. We rafted through
the Canyon awed, but thrilled to terror
when rapids shook our rafts much
as horses shake flies from their shiny
hides. Perhaps most memorable
was Lower Lava (rated 10)

but Hermit and Upset (rated 9)
were monsters, too. Mostly because
I love their names, I keep at heart
the Rancid Tuna, Little Bastard,
and Bright Angel Rapids.

                  Clear
and blue at Lees Ferry, the river
changes after mingling with
the Little Colorado River,
becomes the color and almost
the consistency of peanut butter.
"Bathing" in that goop requires
imagination. When we stopped
at clear wayside falls and creeks
we took full advantage of
their virgin clarity.

                We hiked
through side canyons as grand in their
variety as the Grand itself:
Saddle Canyon where we climbed
over rocks as big as houses
with sheer cliffs rising close
on both sides of tiny us;
Clear Creek with a waterfall
that we could lean against to clean
the Colorado's silt from our pores;
Shinumu Creek where the walls rise
so near and sheer that much of the hike
was in the creek itself; Elves
Chasm with falls and pools inviting
pranks; Blacktail Canyon where

we sat in silence listening
as water drop by drop by drop
by drop by drop informed the world,
but made no dimple in the mirror
we perched around, which showed the cliffs
leaning above us and a notched
rhombus of sky filled with fleecy clouds;
Deer Creek with plunging falls
we stood behind to see the world
through a shining veil; Matkat Canyon
with pools like bathtubs, and flowers, ferns
and grasses like none we'd seen before;
Havasu Creek where carbonate
turns water blue-green and clear
as backyard swimming pools; and others
I've forgotten even with photos to
remind me of their splendors.

The vanished (or ghostly) Anasazi
once occupied a thousand sites
or more, farming the Canyon floor
and storing their harvest high on cliffs
in granaries inaccessible
to enemies and rodents. Field
glasses let us see these structures;
also a broken wooden bridge
hanging where not even big-
horn sheep seem likely to seek a crossing.
In several side canyons we
explored their homes, now tumbled walls
of rock, and saw petroglyphs
they marked their passage with. They must
have been small people or else it is

their children's hands, outlined
with pigment, that appear on walls
sheltered by overhangs of rock.
(Our children made the same
kinds of images in school,
except on paper, not on rock.)
By 1300 AD
the Anasazi left the Canyon,
escaping a lasting drought most likely.
The modern Hopi are their descendents,
and Hopi still return to mine
for ceremonial salt that leaches
from the Tapeats Sandstone walls. .

Ravens always came when the rafts
shoved ashore for meals or tenting.
They stalked about while waiting for
an unattended plate or sandwich.
Bighorn sheep ran and leaped
where we, if climbing, would have had
to pick an apprehensive way,
straining for hand holds and toe
rests. Mule deer, less agile
than the sheep, surprised our wonder
simply by appearing where
they hadn't been a moment before.
Bank beavers, wise enough
not to dam the Colorado
as men have done (and scheme to do
again) felled willows and aspens
for food near our camps. Jays
and canyon wrens, spotted sand-
pipers and rock squirrels, ants

and spiders, scorpions and bees,
dragon flies and damsel flies—
wherever we climbed or rowed or floated,
something living caught our interest.
Once we saw a peregrine
falcon pluck a teal from the air.

All this was Grand, no doubt, but I
am so quirked that what looms
in memory is less the grandeur
than the people, my fellow rafters.

Ray (whose cerebral palsy seemed
to whet his appetite for adventure)
needed help to be sure, but we
who helped him helped ourselves as well.
If it hadn't been for Ray, would we
have achieved community so fast?
Small, knobby—muscled (not
a spare ounce of fat on him)
Ray seemed more fit than most of us.
His gray hair and beard, trimmed
short and bristly, were so appropriate
to our conditions that I convinced
my wife to use her manicure
scissors (the nearest to barber tools
we had) to help me ape his style.
Not till near the end of the trip
could I decipher Ray's difficult
speech, but from the first I knew
the drift of what he said, simply
reading his gray, expressive eyes.
One windy night Ray's tent

collapsed on him and started skidding
riverward with Ray inside
yelling for help. Kathy and Katherine
saved him from drowning.

                      Kathy is
a pro sea-canoeist, strong
enough to save our whole party
if we had needed saving. She
is tall, blue-eyed, blonde and cheerful
(but not full of professional cheer—
she seems as genuine as trees).
She's on the staff of Wilderness
Inquiry, responsible for Ray
but helping all of us extract
the sweet from the Grand Canyon.

Katherine, her life-partner, practices
law, but wanted not to talk
about it: she took the trip to get
away from law. She looked unlikely
as hiker, paddler, camper: round
as Santa's wife, she carried a big
load wherever she went, and she
went everywhere, not always cheerfully.

Tiny Toni never complained,
but neither did she go on all
the hikes. At seventy, she felt
entitled to withhold herself
from folly sometimes. Eliot,
her husband, plunged into all
the trouble he could find—was the first

to run a rapids in "the rubber
ducky," an inflatable kayak.
Eliot and Toni served as social-
work missionaries in
Japan for many years, then taught
in universities. They now
live in retirement with a host
of other former missionaries.
Eliot often escapes from
their community (where he is fit
enough to do those chores too hard
for others) to hike and help maintain
the Sierra Trail. While he's on one
of his adventures, Toni keeps
busy with committee work
and managing a used clothing
"emporium," the profits of which
provide some health insurance for
the oldest missionaries, who
have tiny pensions.
                Both of them
are skiers. See them? Eliot tall
and lanky, Toni short and pudgy
swooping down the snowy slopes
like Don Quixote and Sancho Panza,
he in quest of bold adventures,
she towing commonsense
and motley-proverbed wit along.

Don and Janet, too, embrace
adventure. They told exciting tales
of travels in Tibet and China,
Africa and Russia, where

they counted cranes and studied them
for the International Crane Foundation.
Don taught music till retirement.
Janet was secretary to a dean
at a university. It's Don's
photographs that keep our memories
somewhat honest. (We give ourselves
to the moment, loath to serve a camera.)
They are lovers after a life
together. Don *would* turn to see
that Janet was safe in the paddleboat,
endangering all the paddlers as
he did so. Such is doting love.
But who among us, forced to choose,
would not forsake the world to save
the one we love above all others?

Cactus Bob (so called because
he grasped a cactus once to keep
from falling off a cliff) was small
and droll and gnarly. His theory
about the Anasazi (that they
were exiles from communities
surrounding the Grand Canyon, condemned
to wrest a bleak existence from
that barren, dangerous place) came
to be called "the Penile Justice Thesis"
by other members of the party.
He stuck to it, however, unfazed
by ridicule and laughter, and earned
our grudging admiration so.

Bob and Ron are friends. They met

in college long ago, and make
their livings by ecology,
though not for the same employer. They
did comic patter as ludicrous
as Bob and Ray's, with Bob as straight
man, Ron providing wicked nonsense.
Bob would lecture at the drop
of a stone, and stones were always dropping
on our hikes. (As luck would have
it, no one was injured by them nor
by Bob's uncurbed intelligence.)
Bob and his wife had begun a trip
the year before, but on the second
day his wife had had to be
helicoptered out with a broken
leg. Canyon Explorations
offered them the chance to take
the trip again, paying only what
the rise in price had been. When she
refused the chance, Ron volunteered
to occupy her slot on the roster.
Ron has flesh and flash to spare,
and spends the flash, at least, freely.

Patricia is a court reporter
when not on vacation. She told us once
that when she returned from a brief stint
in Domestic Court to her usual job
in Criminal Court, she celebrated.
"Criminals are nicer," she
reported wryly, "than parties in
divorce proceedings." She is small
and agile, ready for anything.

Her blue eyes sparkle when she talks.

Frank, the Quiet Man among
loquacious people, works for a state
pollution control agency,
and could have told us more than he did
about the world surrounding us.
When asked, he often had the fact
eluding me. He's quiet in
appearance as in manner; I find
it hard to recall an image of
him (except with photos) but his talk
lingers like a mellow tune.

Paul is liaison between
a computer company and schools,
and wishes schools were less concerned
with operating hardware, more
with logic. His employer gives
sabbaticals, and Paul had spent
his last as a volunteer in schools
in South Korea. He was on
his current sabbatical now. He had
the build of a natural athlete and
the temperament of a friendly clown.
We have a picture of him diving
through one of the Elves Chasm falls,
a human cannonball, into
the deep crystal pool below.
We were a friendly, helpful party
overall, but everyone
admired and liked especially Paul.

Alice had wondered if sleeping on
the ground would make arthritic hips
hurt, but claimed it was no problem.
Still, she woke long before
the rest of us, and many of
her journal entries read as scribbles
because they were composed by moonlight
or starlight or in the dark.
She climbed some cliffs that I declined,
and dared try all the tests that we
were offered. She has kept me surprised
for almost fifty years, more
than ever on our Canyon trip.

Garrett, the leader of our party,
is tall, perhaps as much as six
feet-three, and heavy, too (he'd spent
the summer tending the family business,
Canyon Explorations, so put
on extra pounds). But when we saw
him carry Ray in a sort of back-
pack while climbing steep cliffs,
we marveled at his strength and skill.
He worked as hard at everything
as his employees, and seemed to enjoy
the trip as much as his clients did.
Curly-haired, with laughing blue
eyes and fair but sunburned skin,
he drawled directions, information,
stories, always droll but lucid.

Mary Ann (or M.A.
as she prefers) is beautiful

but tough. When rafting through a rapids,
she perched in a sprawling posture,
hands on hips or arms crossed
(while I was hanging on with all
my strength) as if to say that danger
bored her, which it may have done.
Her father, now retired, had been
a diplomat. She spent much time
in Denmark, Paris, the Netherlands
when she was young and her teen years
in a boarding school. (There was a time
I would have envied her upbringing,
but now I'm glad to be excited
and amused as readily as I am.
Boredom seems the worst of wastes
in a wacky world.) She feels as much
at home in the Grand Canyon, she says,
as anywhere, and maybe that
is why she seemed so bored sometimes.

Rachel also spent her youth
in Europe, where her parents taught
in schools for dependents of
the U.S. military. If she
was ever bored, she hid the signs.
As strong as she is beautiful,
she wore a brace on her sprained left wrist,
but rowed a raft as skillfully
as any of the other guides.
(She lent me a glove to wear on the hand
I'd burned before the trip began,
so I was predisposed to love her.
A purple glove it was, and I

look quite the dandy wearing it
in photos.) She had majored in
geology in college, and told
us just enough about the passing
Canyon's features to keep us keen
on learning more. She also rafts
in the Grand Canyon's off-seasons,
in Costa Rica mostly, but once
in Africa on the wild Zambezi.
Tanned to a golden bronze, with freckles
on her nose, she has the greenest
eyes and blackest, thickest lashes
I remember ever seeing. But what
I most remember is her laughter,
infectious as the common cold.

This was Nicki's first trip
since qualifying for a guide's
license. No one rode with her
the first few days. Instead, her raft
was laden with provisions, gear
and beauty. Younger than our youngest
daughter, Nicki glows: though slender,
she has curves where curves should be
and features that are *features*. Joe
Biner said that she was made
to break hearts, and maybe she
was breaking his. She studied in
a school of architecture, hoped
to build the kinds of structures that
are kind to our beleaguered planet.
She shines in conversation as
in beauty, so when Garrett said

that she could carry passengers,
there was a near stampede to her raft.

Joe Biner, I suspect,
knows heart-breaking inside out.
Though cerebral palsy twists his legs
so he can barely walk and makes
him loath to feed himself for fear
of making a spectacle of himself
(or maybe he just wanted to
be fed by Nicki, Rachel, and
M.A.) he handles rafts
as craftily as other guides.
He said that since his muscles are
in constant contests with each other,
in effect he's working out
most all the time, and that accounts
for his impressive, taut physique.
He speaks clearly, but without
the normal tunes of English speech.
To compensate, his language has
the color, pith, economy
and wit of poetry. He told
us stories nearly every night,
supposedly from life, but life
as seen and lived by genius.
He was recovering from cancer,
yet he seemed as carefree
and merry as anyone I've known.
He told us once that his mother's gloom
is one burden he finds hard
to bear: "It seems some people just
aren't meant for happiness," he said.

He makes a Canyon trip but once
or twice a year, when there are folks
with handicaps in a Can-Ex party.
Otherwise he's guiding anglers
and selling them supplies near
Darby, Montana (Norman Maclean
country. He tells amusing tales
about the making of the movie
"A River Runs Through It," for which
he manned a camera raft.) He sees
himself as lucky because his father,
a dentist, is his best friend
and saw that Joe acquired the skills
he needed to become the free
and independent man he is.
When Joe was small, his father would take
him fishing, set him on a rock
in the middle of the river with
a rod and tacklebox, then dis-
appear to wade and cast dry flies
for hours. When he returned
he'd find that (as a rule) his son
had caught some fish. Joe told about
the time he saved allowances
and money gifts till he could buy
his own saddle. His family lived
in L.A. at that time, but Joe
spent his summers on a ranch
in Montana. The year he got his saddle
was the first he flew alone to Missoula,
his saddle in a gunny sack.
His plane was late, the terminal
near empty. No one from the ranch

was there to meet him. "So this nine-
year old cripple found his saddle
going 'round and 'round on the baggage
carousel, and dragged himself
aboard. When Harvey from the ranch
got there, he found me riding 'round
and 'round and yelling, Hi ho, Silver!"

Like Garrett, Larry wore a sash
of fat around his muscular middle.
He'd not be chosen from a line-up
as a river guide, yet rowed
and climbed with more than ample
strength and skill. He had a pompous
air and often told us more
than we required about the passing
Canyon's features. We admired
him, but we rode in other's rafts
when possible. In off-seasons
he's a ski instructor, and owns
a restaurant in Telluride,
Colorado. He seemed to take
more pleasure in the cooking than
the other guides did, and perhaps
more pleasure in the eating, too.

But all of us devoured the food
as if we were the customers
of a four-star restaurant. Perhaps
our burning more energy
than usual gave our appetites
their cutting edge. All the food
needed for twenty-one rafters

for fifteen days rode the rapids
with us, although converted daily
into shit that must be carried
from the Canyon in sealed containers
(surplus ammo canisters).
We peed in the Colorado, then
drew water from the river for
the cooking pots and water bottles,
first of course pumping it
through filters and adding chemicals.
It seemed a little strange to stand
pissing into water not far
from fellow rafters bathing in it,
but we were told the volume of
the river "waters down" the piss
to paltry insignificance.

Nicki may have broken Joe's
susceptible heart, but he was wriggling
into hers. She listened to
his stories eagerly, and talked
with him for hours on end at night.
The last time we rode with her,
she spoke some doubts about her boy-
friend, wondered whether he was too
conservative to make a life with.
She couldn't quite imagine now
how she could be content, wed
to a teacher who liked a smalltown life.

Our last night in the Canyon was
October 1st, and campfires
are allowed then on the sand. We scrounged

some driftwood, twigs and dried weeds,
and after supper sat around
the fire singing and feeling sad—
at least, that's how *I* felt. Though
some of us whose homes were near enough
together laid a makeshift plan
to gather at our home the following
spring, I knew I'd never see
most of them again. The best
of this experience was the way
we fit together, entertained
and helped, listened and felt free
to speak our hearts to one another.
I felt I knew these folks as well
as many I had known for years.

The site where we were camped that last
night was only two hours' rafting
from Diamond Creek, the place where we
would load the rafts and other gear
on a truck, then ride back to Flagstaff.
As we had set our tents up, Joe
predicted rain, although the sky
was clear. He said that it had *always*
rained when he camped there. We laughed
at him.

But as we took our tents
down, easy rain began to fall,
and by the time the rafts were loaded,
we were wet clear through. Alice
asked Joe how it felt always
to be right. "It's a heavy burden,"

he replied, heaving a sigh.
We had no breakfast. The plan had been
to eat a fancy spread the truck
was bringing, and then to load the truck.
But when we pushed ashore at Diamond
Creek, the drivers said we had
to get away before the road
washed out. With Garrett's clear instructions
(and our experience sharing chores)
we did the job in record time.

A couple of the Can-Ex staff
rode with the truck. The rest of us
were loaded into vans and told
not to fasten our seatbelts lest
they trap us if the vans washed
away in the flood. I didn't see
a match to that road until we went
to Monteverde in Costa Rica,
but there the ruts were dry while here
each rut was a fast-running stream.
We bounced around like soccer balls
for fifteen miles, as scared as we
had been in Lower Lava. Here
and there, the road had disappeared
and the vans had to make new tracks.
At last we reached the top and a tarred
road that led to Route 66.

There is
a tourist trap on 66
with menagerie and souvenirs
and "world-famous" junkfood. There

we waited for the truck and banquet.
When they arrived, we ate as if
for the first time in fifteen days.
Any food is comfort food
when you've escaped a raging flood.

Though long showers in our room
were blissful (and real privacy
for love) we looked with pleasure to
the farewell dinner, held in a Flagstaff
restaurant whose name I'm glad
we lost: a noisy, crowded bar
with tiny tables; decent, undistinguished
food; no conversation
really. Maybe that was best.
We gladly left the place and all
our new-made friends, began
to polish up our Grand adventures
recollected here for you
these six years after coming home.

A VOICE IN THE NIGHT

One of several times when I "retired"
from teaching, my senior students celebrated
the episode with a handsome gift, a clock-
and-pen set fit to grace a desk finer
than any I was ever likely to own.
A small gold-plated plaque proclaimed my name
and this seductive hyperbole: "THE GREATEST
from the Class of '63." I modestly
reminded them of Dr. Johnson's counsel:
"Don't accustom yourselves to use big words
for small matters." Though riddled by blind worms,
my core of common sense told me the quote
was all too a propos; but as I read
the golden plaque again and again and again
and again, I began to believe its flattering legend.

Later that summer, one night I sat at my desk—
a rude, over-loaded table that spanned
a window looking on the street—and tried
to nail my attention to the half-completed
poem there; but the clock with its golden motto
pulled my notice to it like a magnet.
A sudden squeal of tires scraped my ear
as a car slid 'round the corner, and a voice cried out,
"Fuck you, Mister La-a-a-a-a-ngwor-r-r-rthy!"
Lanced by the candor of the gleeful voice
my swollen pride shrank till once again
it fit me like my own freckled skin.

THE RESTLESS PROPHET

Hope-infused, the prophet tries
to ply his vision as a lever
to help his supine neighbors rise
before they fall asleep forever.

ON THE WAY, 1970

I see them mostly in the morning,
those crumpled humps of fur
or feather, snared at first by the scornful
stare of truck or car,
then broken as only flesh can break.
Taking the sudden blow on
his flinching mind, the driver felt sick
and ashamed, for a few moments
at least. Even a hunter regrets
this aimless, dirty kill.

Some of the broken bodies were pets
restively on prowl
to reassert their nature. These
are usually found and buried—
if by children, with obsequies
so satisfyingly florid
the loss is temporarily worth
sustaining; if by adults,
with a blind, angry reflexive curse
for the unknown driver, whose faults
are likely no worse than their own.

But most of the victims were wild—
'possum, pheasant, deer, raccoon—
their vital colors spilled
like trash in the road. Why, I have seen
even the vivid, cunning
fox crushed, despite his keen
perceptions and crafty running.

Driving to work through farmlands graced
by woodlots and "idle acres,"
I watch the road for crows. Dressed
like butlers or undertakers
they gather coolly to tidy up.
But when a car approaches,
they cock their heads, then darkly flap
away to prudent perches.
Their rising warns me to slow down
and honor the living fact
the corpse was once. I can't atone.
The crows return to their snack
when I have passed. A few hours later
I eat my lunch with as good
an appetite as theirs, or better.

So why should I find it odd
that the President can flaunt position,
relish football, be
a proud devoted father to Trish and
Julie while daily he
presides over the breaking of bodies?
Like most of us he takes
what cheer he can along the road he's
on. When conscience brakes
us now and then, we wince and mourn,
but few go forth on foot
thereafter. The rest of us may yearn
to live in grace, yet put
our fate (if not our faith) in speed
and comfort. Distance heals
remorse when living creatures bleed
and break beneath our wheels.

THE SOLID CITIZEN READS HIS EVENING PAPER

He reads the paper to confirm his fears,
twisting events till they squeak assurance, then galls
himself with the confirmation. Having wrung
the bitter columns till his vision blears,
he too is wrung: the bile of civil brawls,
of crimes and wars and falsehoods floods his tongue;
like vomit, accusations burn his throat.
If other men were good as he is good
(not perfect, of course—he knows he has his foibles)
if all were content like him to work and vote
and rest in simple pleasures and honor the God
trusted on coins and bills, then how enjoyable
life would be! But human nature, being so various,
makes the solid man's solidity precarious.

SEEN FROM AN
OFFICE WINDOW

A sprinkler, propelled by water pressing through
its mechanism, pulled itself along
the boulevard while swinging silvery arcs
behind, above, ahead, above, behind,
above, ahead, etcetera. "How ingenious!"
I thought, until the rain began to fall
and the sprinkler stalled in a patch of skimpy grass.
Its spiked wheels digging in soon churned
a muddy mess and there the sprinkler sat,
still swinging arcs of water through the rain.
It seemed to be an emblem of some kind.
Maybe you can tell me what it meant?

SAWING APPLE BOUGHS FOR WINTER FIRES

With a sound like fire raging in resinous wood
the crown of the apple tree cracked on a gust
and toppled shivering. First to break was the tall
central bough, which weighed its fellows down
as it sprawled, and snapped our telephone line as well.
A month ago, such a wind would not
have harmed the tree, but laden now with fruit
it fell victim to its own increase.
I took bowsaw and ladder to the wreck
and spent the rest of the afternoon aloft
trying to salvage the tree. A native crab,
its fruit was for the birds; but in the spring
what a bounty of blossoming! Having spent
such sweetness on the scented cloud of bloom
it had none left for the fruit. And when the cloud,
tugged by the wind, let go, it settled on
the lawn like aromatic snowflakes.
But maybe those are purely pleasures of
the past: I saved what foliage I could
hoping the tree can store sunlight enough
this summer to feed it through another long
Minnesota winter. All the same
it was radical surgery I performed: the tree
now stands askew, its truncated limbs
stressing the gap in the back fence-line. It needs
a crutch, or seems to. If it survives this hurt
and takes a chance on growing big again,
I'll trim more boughs next summer to restore
its balance. Ten years from now it may
look whole again. Whoever planted the tree
fifty years ago would understand

the care I took to save it. Why have I never
thought of them with gratitude before?
After the surgery I turned to the yard,
a litter of lopped limbs. The bowsaw set
its eager teeth to the task (a hatchet helped)
and cleaned the larger boughs for firewood.
Alice helped me drag the smaller stuff
to the driveway, which it filled with a wilting hedge
as tall as a man. I saved for another day
the exercise of sawing boughs to chunks
of fireplace length.
                        Now that other day
has come, and almost gone. I spent it mostly
in air-conditioned comfort doing work
that never seems to come to much, to less
at least than most of the folks I try to help
expect and really need. Supper done,
I've come to the yard, shaded by lofty elms
and maples, but hot and humid nonetheless.
With two of the straighter limbs I improvise
a low but solid bed to rest the boughs on
while they are being cut, then fetch the saw.

The bowsaw seems to glide through this green wood.
A chatty cadence. Chainsaws stink and snarl
but if I had one probably I'd use it.
Do the same with the car, driving when
I'd rather walk if only I would think.
Invention is the murder of reflection.
Let's see: this bough will make four long or five
short ones. The applewood we had two years
ago made the finest fires we've ever had.
The smoke was so fragrant! And the flames

displayed every color of the rainbow.
That makes sense: wood is little more
than trapped sunlight that the fire releases.
Wish I could trap the body heat
I'm generating. Maybe I should wait
and saw the wood next winter as we need it,
saw it in the basement. The way I feel
I'd heat the house an hour in minus-zero
weather. Too bad it's wasted. Entropy.
Wonder how much our children will suffer for
the waste my generation's made? Perhaps
they'll be reduced to lives as simple and
complete as Father's was. Not likely, though.
How ludicrous that they may think of ours
as a golden age. Who was it—Thomas Gray?
that didn't care about posterity?
"What did they ever do for me?" That's witty,
but the joke depends on a sense of gratitude
to those who went before and did for us
so much—including all the tasks they left
to challenge us. That's the heritage
we'll hand to our posterity—if we don't
smash the whole shebang, our children with
the rest. More sawdust here than I had reckoned on.
Should have some rich manure to mix with it.
Wish we could raise a few chickens. Maybe
Banties? Tell the neighbors they're only pets.
Or rabbits. Cottontails are getting more
than we from the garden. Cock their heads and crouch
trembling till I can almost touch them, then
they scuttle. Can they tell we'd rather share
with them than do them any harm? We're lucky
to have them here in the middle of the city.

Wonder if we'll ever buy that farm
we dream about? I have to keep my job
at least till all the kids have finished school.
Not that college means as much as we
in our rural innocence imagined. Still,
it opens doors sometimes. Some doors might better
be left shut, like those in Bluebeard's castle.
But ignorance of evils is not the same
as innocence: few of us intend the wrongs
and deaths our selfishness entails.
If I had stayed on the farm, how different would
my life have been? Simple rhythmic tasks
like sawing wood refresh me now, but what
if this were labor instead of leisure? Guess
I'll stop for a cigarette. Dear gracious God,
that sunset! Why did I arrange it so
my back was to the sun? So I could turn
and be amazed by all those colors. Hope
there's rain for us in those kindled clouds.
Dear God, forgive my always wanting more
of everything—except my just deserts!
I've had more luck than anyone deserves
and can't help wondering when the bill comes due.
I'd better get on with this while theres's still light
to see by. Here's a heavy one, enough
to make a winter evening's entertainment.
Wish I knew what kind of owl that is.
Sounds like solemn laughter. The bats are out.
They swoop and veer with such vivid grace
outdoors. Trapped in a room with a bat, do I
reflect its panic or does it echo mine?
Lots of mosquitoes they can catch out here,
and full of my vital juices, too!

Amazing how we feed on one another,
all creatures great and small, and seldom know
ourselves the link between two others in
the cunning chain. We feel it when we're fed
on though! These boughs I've used for props are all
that's left. Lay them on the cut ones now.
Hot as it is, I wish there were more. Greed.
"But how can you know how much is enough until
you've had too much?" A hellish proverb indeed.
Blake himself would reel at the gross excess
we're guilty of. But nature seems inexhaustibly
potent, rising from the ruins we
create. That time out West, driving on
new Interstate. The old abandoned road
ran beside and through the old road plants
were gamely pushing up, some quite large—
the greenest, most hopeful-looking growth
in all that desert drabness. There, all done.
I'll wait till tomorrow to split and stack it in
the shed.

                         "Alice! Come see the moon!"

MISSING TEETH

Exploring with my tongue the palpable gap
between my canines, I recall the dark
backward and abysm of time. To be
again a baby (toothless, dependent, close
to—is it God?) I only need to live
long enough. Already well on the way,
I loathe the disembodied grin I bought
to mask my unfitness as predator.
To hold my own (and get more) I must
put in those Cheshire choppers every day
and bare them in that gracious threat we call
"a smile" (one cannot smile incisively
without incisors). What I'd really like to do
is bravely go without them, show the world
a friendly, graceless, harmless grin beneath
the battered crown and floppy brim of my
fedora. But vanity is dislodged
less easily than rotten teeth. Beside,
it's really not enough to do no harm.
One has to give and take, consume, create
live in the actual world. Speaking plainly
(something else one cannot do without
incisors) false teeth are quite as true
as toothless hankering for innocence.

THE EXPECTED DOESN'T
ALWAYS HAPPEN

All day the wind has toiled, packing clouds
into denser, darker, bigger bundles
and shifting them from shoulder to shoulder.
Another glum weekend coming up.

Expecting to be drenched, ready to run,
I walk sourly homeward.

What's this?
The wind has squeezed the clouds in its fists,
daftly, deftly squirting sunshine on me!

ADVICE ABOUT RASPBERRIES

Thirsty plants, they'll grow in any well
drained soil, but too much fertilizer does
them in. One type of cane bears fruit just once,
mid-summer, then it dies; another bears
in early fall and then again in June
before it dies, whereon you prune it from
the row. Oenophiles will rave about
a vintage hinting of the taste and scent
of raspberry; but if you prefer
the full fragrance to subtlety, you can
make splendid wine of raspberries themselves.
It's best to pick them while the sun is high,
for late in the afternoon half-ripe ones half-
hidden by leaves may fool you with their rouge:
you tug at one and find you've broken off
a whole cane-tip, and so lose the green
ones clustered 'round the flirt. But take your time
while picking and you won't make such mistakes:
a berry's ripe if it lets you unbutton it
without fuss or fidget. Don't drop the best
ones into the berry box, but press them on
your tongue and taste the season's glorious essence.

APRICOTS

I never cared for apricots until
I plucked one ripe and sun-warmed from a tree
and bit into that juicy sundrop. O
Eve! It was no apple tempted you!
In California's Central Valley they grow,
of course, like everything; but when we moved .
to Minnesota we discovered wise
and patient horticulturists have grown
varieties that bear even here—
at least some years. I must have planted twelve
trees at two homes in this arBoreal
state, but only three have rewarded my
enthusiasm. Even they surprise
us when they bloom. One day in April
all the trees, including native plums,
are bare (there may be snow still on the ground);
then we come home to find blushing blossoms
adorning the busy limbs of apricots.
Experience has taught us not to set
our hopes too high, to take our pleasure from
the blooms themselves (as we are wont to do
when candidates we favor speak good sense):
a late sharp freeze is all too likely to nip
the nascent fruit (as like as sense to go
against the grain of popularity).
Still, our apricots do bear some years,
and when they do we never rue our work
in helping them. They taste as they promise: true
embodiments of the sun's munificence.

SUNRISE, MOONSET:
FEBRUARY 1, L980

(for Alice)

The full amber moon
paused on the western rim
of the snowy world just as
the sun arose in the east,
bold as only the sun
dare be. Did she bow then
before his potency
or flee from it? Perhaps
the drowsing groundhog knows,
for whom the sun and moon
dance a winter's dream.
But you and I, transfixed
in snow by the rare glance
between those peerless lights,
joined mittened hands
to go a wondering way
through the cold new morning.

FALLING

We lay in the hammock, your head on my shoulder,
my arm holding yours to warm
us both in the starry chill of August
midnight. Above, the heavens swayed
and sang: the moon a mere whisper,
the stars a multitudinous choir.
And though we were there to watch for them
the Perseids flashed across our sight
like pheasants rising from tall grass
at a hunter's feet, surprising us
too much for us to interate
the magical *moneymoneymoney*.
"Why wish for a fortune anyway?"
you said. "We've everything we need."

Excepting faith that mankind has
a future. We should wish, O Perseus!
Fire those flaming arrows at
our modern gorgons! Slay them in
their silos!

                    But if wishes were horses
I would ride the winged one sprung
from Medusa's gushing blood, not sit
cheerless before an open window
chilled by a prosing breeze and thoughts
of missile madness while you, dear muse,
lie alone in our double bed.

A moment ago a tiger lily
dropped all its petals at once

plop! on the cluttered coffee table.
Fallen flowers, fallen stars,
fallen men. Yet there are stars
still in their courses, flowers in bud,
and men may fall through the web of fears
and brags and dares they've spun to find
themselves at last upon the stairway
hope, climbing into love.

JANUARY VIGIL

Having fed the glowing heap of coals
a few chunks of oak, I linger in
the window-bay to watch the wind raving.
Our yard is like a seething cauldron, snow
writhing up in furious, hairy clouds.
On such a night the world flies upside down
and backwards. Nothing lasts for long out there
except the whale that's rising in our garden.
He breaches every winter, phoenix-like,
a bold answer seeking for its riddle.

I shiver, shaking off the giddy spell
cast by the seething yard and whale, and try
to make out lights along the highway where
half an hour ago Alice and I were driving—
or being driven. Such a wind gores
a car, then lifts and shakes its massive head.
Waiting to be flung into a ditch,
one almost hopes that it will happen soon
to end the agony. To be *somewhere,*
even in a ditch, seems safer than
to wonder where the road has gone. A few
winters ago, caught in such a storm,
we had the wind at our backs driving the snow
past us into the blank white future.
Feeling as if the car was in reverse
I kept looking back to see where we were going.
A jack-knifed semi stopped us that time. We spent
that night and all the following morning waiting
(with other travelers trapped behind us) waiting
for the wind to weary of its sport. At last

a fellow in a 4 X 4 pickup
picked us up along with several others
and somehow got us to the next town,
Zumbrota, where we spent another day
and night before the storm grew bored by its own
performance. How that fellow in the pickup
found his way I'll never know: all I
could see were obstacles obscured by snow:
abandoned trucks and cars and headhigh drifts
and one snowplow plunged in ignominy.

Although it feels as if the roof may fly
before this night is done, our family
are home together, feeling safe and grateful.
But others out there yet (some we know
and love, some we only pity) deserve
a vigil—pointless almost certainly,
for neither prayer nor pity reaches them.
But how can we deny a claim that helps
us mirror God, whose eye is on the sparrow
even as the hawk stoops?

PISSING ON THE PAST

I

Starting at the small-town school my sister
and I had walked to and from in all
weathers (but mostly, as I recall, in snowstorms)
I set out to show my wife the farm
from which I once escaped only to dream
and lie about its splendors ever after.
My first mistake: we drove instead of walking.
Nothing was as far as everything
once seemed. In no time we left the town
behind and turned from the gravel township road
into a cloud of dust our car had raised.
We headed down the seldom-traveled lane
that led to the farm. But where were the wild plum.
alder and cherry thickets that once had lined
the lane? Those natural hedges—full of flitting,
scolding, trilling birds—had set our home
apart, had made of it a private world
that lured lovers: often, returning late
at night, we had to wait while parked cars
blocking the narrow lane got under way,
then follow them as they fled ahead of us
the whole embarrassing way to our yard
where there was room to turn and exit quickly.
One memorable moonlit night, our headlights flushed
a naked couple from the couch they had made
by taking out a seat from their sedan.
Mother tried to keep us kids from watching
the silent-movie rush to dress and put
the seat back in and leave, but all her efforts
only kept her from seeing the show herself.

The lane was now a meager grassy track
between two fields of corn. I slowed the car
to a pace approximating that of kids
reluctant to get home and do their chores.
We loitered around the looping curve that starts
the steep descent into the river valley
and saw, where buildings had been, nothing but corn.
The drafty stucco house, once tucked against
a hill, had vanished. Even the terrace it
had occupied was gone, bulldozed to
oblivion. The massive barn, built into
another hill, had not quite disappeared:
its crumbling limestone walls now sheltered charred
timbers and twisted metal roofing. Corn
was planted to within a tractor's breadth
of the wasting walls. But what amazed me most
and most dismayed me: where the artesian well
had gushed its never-ending icy stream—
corn, nothing but corn. The willow-lined
brook that once had borne the overflow
(marvelous for dams and waterwheels!)
how could that be gone? And all those elms
and cottonwoods and oaks and hawthorn trees?
The marsh behind the well where waterfowl
had fed and rested, spring and fall, now drained,
and all that rare and various life replaced
by corn, for which there is so little need
that politicians labor to contrive
new follies all the time to squander it.
We sat amid the alien corn awhile,
then turned the car around. As I had gladly
left that place long, long ago
I left it gladly now. You can't go home

again: there is no *there* there anymore.

II

My family left that rented river farm
To "get ahead." Father had more than earned
the right to farm a better place, though not
his own: he'd still be share-cropping for
another dozen years, but now we'd have
indoor plumbing, furnace, electric power,
level fields that didn't wash away but did
let us farm with tractors. And there was land
enough to raise a family yet save
some money. Mother's life would be no more
than twice as hard as city women's now.
A school bus ran a few steps from our
front door, and though I now did far
more fieldwork and tending livestock, I was saved
from toting water and firewood. And I
could read till midnight when I chose to do so:
each of us had a room of our own—with lights!
It was a long time before the river farm
acquired its golden glow in memory.

III

About ten years ago my sister came
from California for her fortieth class
reunion. My brother and I drove her there
(a matter of eighty miles or so) and, with
the best intentions, drove her past the farm
we all remembered as a handsome place
with most of the comforts most folks now expect.
We should have known better. The land has been
consolidated with another farm

(or two or three) and though the house is there,
it is no home these days. The roof has fallen.
Scrawny young trees, mostly walnuts,
grow amid the tumbled, rotting wreckage.
The lawn and gardens Mother took such pride in
bloom with abandoned cars and trucks and farm
machinery. Burdocks, nettles, common dock
and other thrifty weeds luxuriate among
vehicular ruins. Could we have found a more
discouraging way to start a celebration?

IV

Nostalgia isn't what it used to be:
what's gone is gone indeed, and gone because
no one thought it paid to keep it.
That ol' cash nexus has us in its spell,
that ol' cash nexus that we weave so well,
though little else we make lasts long at all.

JONATHAN SWIFT:
TO A WASP ALIGHTING
ON HIS BOOK

Your legs adraggle like bits of string,
your blurred wings embrangling the room
with a noise like nothing alive—in flight
you seemed a lost, senseless thing.
But alighting on my book you become
as domestic, self-assured, polite
as any man—and as ready to sting,
no doubt. Now, tell me why you have come.
What? No requests? You slight me,
Sir! Why, once on a time the King
himself used me. There must be some . . .
dog you would have me bite
for you? Or perhaps you would have me sing
your praises? No? You build your home
of paper, don't you? How clean and light
and witty! I may have seen it swing
on a branch of a windy day: a dome
inverted. I suppose you would fight
to keep this new-found province? Wrong!
There you go. You are not Rome
or England: your appetite
has limits, while men, from beggar to King,
covet more the more we consume,
unsatisfied till we inherit Night.

STREET SINGER

A frayed and fragrant fellow trolls
a ditty, key and color off.
A passing woman wrinkles her nose
in disgust, but the singer enjoys, enough
for both, the wretched noise he makes.

THE CONCRETE FINDS ITS FORM

Like Ammons hanggliding slipsliding
skateboarding through a poem, we had
to improvise when the forms (so carefully set
I'd thought) began to give (O treacherous gift!)
before the fluid pressure of concrete.
"Shut that damn thing off!" (A man in trouble
has little use for *please*.) Maybe a few
more stakes—but where's the maul? "Help me push
this planking in—here, use this as a lever.
Hold it there while I . . ." Wham! Wham!
We got the stakes in place and finished pouring,
ending with a graceful, chancy curve
I never would have dared to try achieving.

TRUE POETS

Never seeming to repeat themselves
brown thrashers had been singing from that
pale half-hour before the sun comes up
to suppertime, when Alice and I
sat in the porch-swing just to listen.
"Do they ever take time out to eat?"
she asked. "They're true poets," I replied,
"neglecting all appetites but one."

Unlike me. Whenever food and drink,
friends or love, even heavy work
or weeding gardens offer distraction from
the life-trying, death-defying urge
to sing, I'm likely to heed their lure.
Who would listen, anyway, to me
while brown thrashers maken melodye?

.

FORTY YEARS LATER

If I had known, those many years ago,
how prime a number you are, even I
might have lacked the nerve to ask your hand
in marriage (calculating you would throw
your other hand, your breasts, your lustrous eyes,
your mind—in short, your undivided and
prodigious all—into the deal as well).
My nescience (not without a parallel,
for I am much like other men) was pure
good fortune—the best in what must be
accounted as a very lucky life.
I wanted you was all I knew for sure,
and you agreed this far: to share with me
your far-too-much-to-merely-be a wife.

PRAYER FOR SIMPLICITY

That we may learn to live on less, take
no more from Gaia than she can safely spare,
leave for other creatures everywhere
and for the future what they'll need to make
their lives complete—this is now our prayer,
dear Christ. Nor can we safely wait to learn
this hard lesson, for every daily turn
of Gaia finds her needing to repair
more wounds our wasteful ways inflict. We mourn
those wounds, dear Christ, and humbly pray that you
help simplify our wantings and undo
our folly. So may the world be reborn
a new Jerusalem where everyone
delights to share all blessings under the sun.

AT THE STRAND BOOKSTORE

Shelf on shelf on shelf of poems by poets
I have never read nor even heard of—
stranded here. Perched like an eager bird of
prey, I swoop on a volume, sadly blow its
dust off, start to read, discover grace
and wit and life itself. Then swoop again,
devour another life. Another. When
the wobbly ladder proves too pinched a space
to bear my much-too-much augmented self,
reluctantly I descend. I cannot read
them all nor even sample each. Indeed,
for those I've chosen I must add a shelf
or two our nest will barely accommodate.
O stranded poets, how eagerly you wait!

TINNITUS ON THE POT

Straining on the stool
I'm sometimes disconcerted to find
the crickets' chorus in my skull
swelling to flood my mind.
Their customary song
can be ignored. I seldom hear it.
Only when I try to prolong
a silence, still my spirit
for meditation, does
the crickets' homely diapason
irk me with its constant buzz,
its uninvited brazen
stridulation. Then
I name it, and it slowly fades
away to background music. When
their tedious serenade
most incommodes me, though,
is when it swells and swells and swells
till all I am allowed to know
is what the crickets tell.

but having almost died one time
from blocked bowels, I
rank shitting near as high as rhyme
and reason, though not so high
as many politicians rank it.

SPRING FLOOD

He strolls along a shabby, yet burgeoning street
and tries lazily to bring to mind
the ardors of younger Springs. A greening wind
harries Winter's disorderly retreat,
rattling the sticky buds unfurled by trees
whose roots have pushed the sidewalk into waves.
Ahead of him an ancient woman braves
the wind and April's other treacheries.
Dressed all in black, except her troubled hat
where starchy roses form a snowy wreath,
she slowly makes her way against the breath
of Spring. Unwilling to accommodate
his pace to hers, yet also loath to pass
and leave her struggling in his discourteous wake,
he pauses to consider: should he shake
his diffidence? Summon up the brass
to offer her the comfort of his arm
and conversation? But stays instead to rest
and watch two robins obey the old behest.
They couple quick, then share a hapless worm—
each appetite no sooner waked than sated.
Simplicity itself, and yet they too
are tools of time and will discover soon
how craftily the future is created.

Bells, shouts, shrieks of laughter shatter
his reflection. School's out. Engulfed by a crowd
of escaping teens, like a charred stump by a flood,
the crone disappears in the swelling clatter.
Their elders' vision left behind in school,
the headlong teens don't see the drowning beldame,

and wouldn't hear her if she tried to tell them
anything: to them the past is nil.
Quick and passionate as birds taking
under their wings the lilting Spring that Is
(as who should not?) the colorful deluge flows
around him now in waves that rush toward breaking.

LIVING LIGHTNING RODS

Planted many years before we moved
here, intended to become lightning rods,
our cottonwoods have served their purpose well.
One sustained a dozen strikes before
a bolt tore the last of its living crown
apart and scattered thick furrowed bark
across the yard. The other two, standing
close enough to seem one tree, each
had three major branches thrusting out
and up, twenty feet above the ground.
I couldn't tell which were the central boles
except that the highest ones were lightning-struck
and lost their crowns and bark to winds over
several summers. Two bare stubs of branches
bleakly stand beside the living four.
Without their sacrifice our house might well
have boomed and bloomed with lightning fire.

Visiting an uncle once, we found him in
his grove stripping bark from a tree with an ax.
Nearby, a half-grown steer lay dead. "That calf
was healthy yesterday," my uncle said.
"Lightning must have struck him in that storm
last night, but you can never trust suspicious
insurance men to see the obvious."

HEAVEN'S KILN

(For Richard Bresnahan)

Leaving the St. John's Pottery late
one afternoon in late November, we saw
a western sky more colorful than, but less
natural-seeming than the pots we'd been
admiring. Responsible and witty, the potter tries
to live and work in harmony with nature.
The sun that fired those clouds cares not a fig
for the natural order nor for morals as we
imagine them. Centered like his clay
on the turning earth, the potter plans for the next
three-hundred years and builds the finest pots
he can. The sun consumes itself in burning.
Even when we are turned away, it burns.

VARIETIES OF HUMAN ART

(For Jim Kern)

Some art pokes us in the eye with a sharp
wit and some just hangs there like a damp
dishtowel (we hope it made something shine,
if only the while of its maker's time).
Some art stirs us with a rhythmic hand,
and some, like wind swaggering through a tall
grass prairie, makes our senses sway and stagger.
Some art embodies chunks of the world
and some attenuates the world till it
becomes no more than vastly vacant form.
And some art spins and spins its web
till, running out of thread, it stops.

A QUAKER MEETING
WITH CAT

The Meeting settles into silence; Friends
invite the Spirit. *Speak to me and lead*
me from my selfish self into that
good light where all Thy creatures shine, where ends
are compassed by Thy means, and where Thou
feed my charity with thine. A pacing cat
patrols the Meeting, going from Friend to Friend
on fog feet, asking to be blessed or petted.
Most oblige. The cat contentedly
subsides into a pool of sunshine. *Lend*
me Thy sweet grace, O Spirit, to calm my fretted
life; yet wake me to the duties I
so easily forget. Content to doze
the cat, awash in holy sunlight, glows.

WHY THE OLD MAN SLEPT IN HIS CHAIR

An ancient man who slumbered in his chair,
his head a-bobbling here and there,
replied, when scolded for it, "I don't care.
I haven't energy to spare
for donning nightclothes and climbing into bed.
For all that trouble I'd like as not be dead.

Although I don't expect to live forever
I feel no urgency to sever
the ties that bind me to this blind endeavor
life—no urgency whatever.
I once believed I'd kill myself before
I'd settle for being a wreck on a rocky shore,

but living is living, even when reduced
to this. No genius like Proust,
I nonetheless remember what a boost
I got from doing all I used
to do and knowing folks I see no more.
There's much to mull and wonder at before
I leave this rocky shore."

SUMMER IN THE WINTER
OF OUR LIVES

An electric fan labors on
our bedroom window sill.
Night-cooled air from the sleeping gardens
freely flows between us.
I summon up those short but long-gone
smoldering summer nights
in Hanford, California, where
we didn't own a fan
nor notice much the noisy sweat
that gushed like glue between us.
Yet now I love you more than I
then had the patience for.

VALENTINE

In the time that's coming, dear, when you or I
begin the steep descent or climb to Light
or Darkness, will you still be my Valentine?
If so, I dare believe that I can cope.
As we together have lived with cold and snow—
filling our home with greenery, flowers, and hope,
and feeding birds that have no fear of flying
even when the air is chill as death—
so shall we together live with dying.

PRAYING WITH MOTHER

None of us moved fast enough for you
when we were young—not even Dad could keep
the pace you set. "Get a move one," you
would say, trotting with two full pails of water
or an armful of wood, and we would try.
Now you shuffle down the corridor
of the nursing home, leaning into your walker,
and tell us, "Go ahead, you kids. Don't wait
for me. I'll get there eventually."
(Being called a kid at seventy
more than merely amuses—it delights me.)

You knew the lives of hundreds—friends
and family, neighbors, mere acquaintances—
and told the world whatever you had learned,
but not maliciously. You wanted to
have only good to tell—unless someone
had injured you or those you loved, but then
look out! Your anger never lacked the words
it needed. Now the same bit of news
surprises you again and again in an hour's
palaver. Having heard that so-and-so
has died, you later ask how he or she
is doing, and later still if we have heard
how he or she is taking this bad weather.

Remembering only the good years in your home,
you wish we hadn't moved you here where time
drags its feet and nurses interfere
in your affairs but don't intuit what
you want or think you need. Your clothes

and other chattels disappear—no doubt
stolen, you believe. And when we find
a missing item where you "never would
have put it," those who took it must have brought
it back, knowing you suspected them.

Mother, I join your earnest daily prayer
that God shall take you soon and unaware.

THE LAST ONE CHOSEN

Having pledged my body to a School
of Medicine so that fledgling doctors can
acquire a solid feeling for their craft,
I expect to entertain as well as teach.
Gawky, freckled, haystack-haired, I
endured a lot of taunting laughter as
a boy. When playground heroes chose their teams
I hovered, hopeful but expecting at last
to hear, "Okay, I'll take Langworthy
since he's the one that's left." When made the butt
or wit or witlessness, I learned not
to flinch or carry grudges. I feel I'm ready
to lie on the slab or table, calm as a corpse,
no matter what the students say about
my shriveled (maybe even shriven) body.
When I became a man, I learned to trust
my lean and graceless body. It's done as much
work as well as any athlete's has,
and served as well in loving, too. From what
I hear about those playmates from my youth,
I wouldn't be surprised to hear God
sometime say, "Okay, I'll take Lang-
worthy, since he's the one that's left."

.

PART FOUR
Among Friends

AMONG FRIENDS

Prologue

From 1998 to 2000 the Iglesia de los Amigos en El Salvador and the Northern Yearly Meeting of the Religious Society of Friends were mutually exploring the possibility of a "sister" relationship. Attending international meetings of Quakers, my wife Alice and I had met many Spanish-only speaking Friends, including Maudiel Arevello-Espinoza, pastor of the Quaker Church in Soyapango, El Salvador. We had as little Spanish as they had English, and decided to repair our deficiency. We signed up for a 3-weeks course in San Jose, Costa Rica, and prepared for that with language tapes and drills. Since we would be in the area, we decided to come home by way of El Salvador. We hoped to know enough Spanish by that time to converse with Friends and to learn about the Quaker school and clinic in Soyapango.

We were much too optimistic about our talent for learning Spanish. When we arrived in El Salvador we could manage only primitive conversation with natives who spoke no English. If it had not been for the patient generosity of the Friends community, we would have been lost. There was more than the language barrier to cross: the Northern Yearly Meeting is composed of Monthly Meetings that are unprogrammed, unpastored, and uncomfortable about proselytizing. The El Salvador Junta Annual is composed of evangelical churches with pastors, programs, and steady missionary efforts. Nonetheless, the sister relationship is now established. The two Yearly Meetings exchange visitors regularly, and are learning much from one another.

Alice and I found our time among Salvadoran Friends to be among the most intense, enlivening, and happy experiences of our lives. When very destructive earthquakes struck El Salvador a year after our visit, we worried as if for family. We were not surprised to learn that the Quaker community adopted many children orphaned by the earthquakes.

To make these poems I drew from Alice's travel journal as well as mine. I wrote the poems to help keep our experiences alive for us, and to share them with others.

SATURDAY

The Hotel Princess, home away from home
to Presidents and high muck-a-mucks
in general, including generals. (The travel agent
in San Jose claimed it was the only
place that she could find for us.) We tell
the staff to watch for the bag that hasn't come
on our plane, a fact we learned after
several boring hours in several lines.

                              Our room
gives views of mountains. After rest and showers,
we call the Quaker church, are told that Maudiel
tried to pick us up at the airport
but thought, when we did not appear, we must
have missed our flight. (Those tedious baggage lines!)
It seems we've been expected to stay with Friends.
We tell the woman on the phone that we
have·paid for our hotel for tonight and so
will stay the night and catch a taxi in
the morning to the church. She asks us to call
later when they have had a chance to plan
for our disrupted visit.

                      We spend an hour
making love (more privacy than we
have known in several weeks—more comfort, too).
We shower again, and call the church once more.
The same woman answers, says someone
will pick us up at 8:30 in
the morning. Hungry now, we go downstairs
to check the Princess restaurants, then leave
to find, we hope, El Salvadoran food.

But all we find is European cuisine.
We eat Italian (good) and wander back
to our hotel through streets as bland as any
we recall from any place we've been.
Though it is only nine, we go to bed
and fall asleep at once.

                        The phone breaks
our slumber. What? Morning already? No!
It can't be! And isn't. After much
misunderstanding on the phone, I hear
what sounds like a rumbling echo in the hall
outside our room, and realize the man
on the phone is standing just outside our door.
I use the peephole. A man and woman, he
using a cell-phone, wait there. I tell
them we will open up in uno minuto.
I struggle into trousers (I always sleep
like Adam before the Fall) while Alice finds
a skirt to wear beneath her nightie (a long
T-shirt, gift from admiring granddaughters,
emblazoned with the legend: WOMEN'S SEWING
CIRCLE AND TERRORIST SOCIETY).

I open up and ask the couple in.
They hesitate (awkward silence) then step
barely inside the door. The man
is tall and has a generous gut and friendly
smile; the woman, dark and plump,
looks vaguely worried, but also smiles.
They watch us closely, speak slowly,
gesture broadly to help us get
their meaning. She is Lidia, Maudiel's
sister, and he Jose, her husband. They have come
to make sure we understand that they
will come for us tomorrow, Sunday, to take

us to the church. Embarrassed, Lidia says
we shouldn't have opened the door so readily: even
the Hotel Princess may be host to malos.
We thank them. Yes, we understand that we
should be checked out and waiting at 8:30.

When they have gone, we fall on the bed laughing,
and can't sleep till we have laughed and laughed,
speculating just how shocked they were
by our attire, and laughed some more.
(We learn on Sunday that Soyapango is
an hour's drive from the Princess. They are Friends
indeed, and we regret having laughed,
though as we come to know them better, we
suspect that they laughed their whole way home.)

SUNDAY MORNING

The Quaker church in Soyapango sits
on a hill and is surrounded by tall trees
and a playground (the Quaker school and clinic
share the space). As we approach the church
we hear a jazzy combo playing hymns—
electric keyboard, drums, guitar. It takes
a minute to recognize "What a Friend
We Have in Jesus." Catching it, I think:
how well their style suits the sentiment!
Conducted slowly to the front row
of pews, exchanging greetings on the way,
we feel the awkwardness of celebrity.
But when a man offers us a hymnal, showing
with his finger where they are, we join the song
and settle in as Friends. A boy and then
a girl sing solos, backed by the jazzy combo.
Maudiel arises, introduces us
to the congregation, a flock of friendly faces.
He reads a Bible passage. Another hymn.
We go to Sunday School, the men and women
in separate classrooms. *Los caballeros* sit
in a circle of folding chairs in silent prayer,
then pass a Bible so that each can read
aloud from *Ephesians.* Maudiel discusses
its meaning for our lives and asks that each
man shed his own light on Paul's dispatch.
Regrettably, I only understand
a bit of what they say, these men with work-
hardened hands and shy, tentative voices.

I feel inadequate in every way
to speak, say only "*Gracias por sus bondad.*"

Back in the Meeting room, we're led again
to a frontrow pew. A boy, nine or ten
years old, slides up beside me, says, "*Mi nombre
es David tambien!*" And he adopts me as
his friend because we share a name. We sing
another hymn, and Lidia speaks, her good
humor shining through her devotion. We sing
another hymn. Then Maudiel begins
to preach. I wonder why the microphone?
Trying hard, I almost think I know
what he is saying—now and then, at least,
but tire of making such an effort. In
my home Meeting in Minnesota, Friends
are gathered in the Silence, waiting for
whatever may to happen: sometimes little,
sometimes everything that matters most.

Maudiel's homily, melodious
river, washes over and around me,
swelling, falling, swelling. David, my new-found
friend, is rapt.. I feel the gathering of
the congregation into one Spirit,
borne like me on this flood of fluency.
Ninety minutes later I begin
to understand how George Fox held
a crowd in thrall to his eloquence for hours,
even as their empty stomachs growled.

SUNDAY AFTERNOON

Lidia asks us will we go with her
and Jacqueline to a village ninety kilo-
meters away, where there's a recently formed
Quaker congregation. It will be
a chance for us to see the countryside
and make new Friends among another flock.

Competitive Quaker, Lidia burns the two-
lane asphalt highway, jammed with Sunday traffic.
When on-coming traffic thins for a bit,
she passes as many cars as she dares—more
than I would dare. When someone passes her,
she floorboards the pedal, discontent
till her rival dwindles in the rearview mirror.
Her daughter Jacqueline, torn between glee
and fear, chides her mother through smiling, gritted
teeth. Not having had a ride like this
since rafting through Lava Rapids, we hold hands
tightly, think: "At least we'll die together."

From time to time squads of soldiers dressed
in camouflage, rifles at ready, emerge
from densely wooded slopes or sugar cane
fields. I ask what they are doing there,
and Jacqueline replies, "Just wasting money!"
Has any of our client states not aped
too well the foolish model we provide?
Well, yes: there's wise and only Costa Rica.
No other nation dares disband its army,
preserving peace by serving its people well.
To our right, maybe twenty miles away,
a range of mountains rises, each peak

distinct like mountains in children's drawings.
Some have slightly flattened tops. I half-
expect to see a plume of smoke appear
from one of them, announcing cataclysm.
The countryside, spectacularly green
and beautiful, suggests abundance, but
its people live in mean adobe huts
scattered through the verdant fertile fields.
Perhaps it is enough for them that they
are beautiful and live in paradise?

At the new *Evangelistica Amigos Iglesia*
(a house) a small, shy, comely woman
greets us at the door, a little girl
peeking from behind her skirt. We're here
to show a video, *Jesus*, to the new
congregation. Now and then a child
comes in, or sometimes two or three, a few
accompanied by mothers. Time now
for quiet talk and noisy scrambling play.
After an hour or so, with eight women
and twenty children gathered, Lidia starts
the video, which we watch only till
the Virgin, consorting with a spectral figure,
gets with Child. We leave the children and
their mothers to puzzle out the old
but ever-new mysterious story as
we start back home to Soyapango.

Lidia, *Deo gracia*, drives with care:
the traffic is like rushhour in LA.
Policias abound, pulling drivers off
with who knows what, if any, rationale?
Mistrustful of their ministrations, I
am grateful, also: maybe we'll survive
this bracing adventure in evangelism!

SUNDAY EVENING

We drive through much of San Salvador
to reach this gorgeous view: the city spread
beneath us, lights spangling velvet hills.
Lined with small cantinas (jerry-built
of studs and corrugated metal, picnic
table seating) the street is famous for
pupusas: thick tortillas filled with meat
and crispy slaw, sparked with fiery peppers.
Jose's impressive gut accommodates
impressive quantities. He tells us proudly
that he and laughing Lidia will celebrate
their twenty-fifth anniversary
next month. I tell him we will celebrate
our forty-fifth in June, and they at first
believe I have misspoken, have me count
the years on fingers, are amazed
to find I spoke the number right. Apparently
they thought us younger (or they may have thought
us like those exotic *norteamericanos*
that spend their lives in serial marriages).

We talk of family, theirs and ours. They have
an older son, who teaches in a Friends'
school eighty miles away, and two
grandchildren. When we tell them we admire
as well as like the son and daughter we
have spent some time with, they restrain their pride,
make light of all their children's skills and virtues:
How we manage to communicate
with our slippery grasp of Spanish and their
lack of English shows how well good will
and patience serve. It also helps that we
properly appreciate *pupusas.*

MONDAY MORNING

When we awaken, Jose has gone to work.
Lidia and Jackie soon leave together,
Lidia to her job in a medical lab
after dropping Jackie at her school.
While we shower, Douglas prepares our breakfast:
plantains fried in more grease than Alice
tolerates, cornflakes in hot milk,
and mangoes good enough to make my day.
Student at a university, Douglas
slept last night in a hammock in the carport
so we could have his room. His English,
better than our Spanish, lets us have a real
but easy conversation (easy for *us*).

A slender version of his father, he
was disappointed yesterday when Uncle
Maudiel expected him to leave
a soccer game to help with missionary
work. He wishes he had more time to play
both soccer and his guitar. He's spent some time
in California (maybe missionary work?)
and after graduating with his degree
in computer sciences, he'd like to go
again.

At 7:30 Maudiel
arrives to take us to his home. His wife
Aminda is fixing breakfast. From the way
the table's set it's clear they thought that we
would eat with them. We explain that we have eaten,
but partly from politeness and partly because

the fruit glows in its bowl as if lit from within,
I eat an orange. Maudiel escorts
us to the spare bedroom, reached by going
on the patio and up a flight of stairs
made of welded re-rod. He warns
us not to drink the water from any taps:
it isn't safe and won't be made safe
till those who bottle water lose their clout
with politicians, who thrive on bribery.
He has to go to work now. (Though pastor of
a Quaker church, he makes his living at
another job.) Aminda will take us to
the school and clinic soon, but we have time
to unpack and settle in.

                              Aminda calls
us minutes later, demonstrates
tilting the 5-gallon jug of water
in its ingenious harness to get a glassful.
She repeats the warning Maudiel just gave us.
She tries her English, but returns to Spanish
quickly. Good at reading our expressions,
she's also good at finding alternate ways
to get her points across.

                         A 5-minutes'
drive to the school. Perhaps sixty children
on the playground, swinging, sliding, playing
tag and other running games. Dressed
in light blue shirts and dark blue skirts or trousers,
they fly and swoop and swirl, their voices light
and joyful. Little groups run over to hug
Aminda and check us strangers out, then wheel
away to play till shrill whistle blasts
call them to their classrooms (the ones used
by the Sunday School). Aminda leads us to

each classroom, starting with the youngest children,
four to six years old. They greet us with giggles
and *"Buenos dias!"* shouted in unison.
The rooms are crowded and spare compared to those
we volunteer in back home, but the harried
teachers there would love to teach these children:
attentive, well-behaved, responsive, neat.
The older children, having studied English
several years, now show their skill: "Good morning!
Welcome to your house!" (*Mi casa es
su casa.*) They revert to Spanish to
recite a lesson in geography
(one class). Another reads aloud, by turns,
from shared textbooks, two children to each
book.

Aminda takes us to the office
where she explains the fees: the lowest is
$10 per month, not enough
to cover all the costs but more than some
families can easily spare. Because
the public schools have sixty to sixtyfive
children in a class and, often, no
books or materials, parents sacrifice
to send their children here and make sure
they buckle down to honor their good fortune.
We're taken to the Meeting room to wait
till all the children in the school arrive
singing, offkey but lustily,
bright and beautiful as birds in a rain
forest. They shout, "Welcome to your house!"
The older children sing a special song
adorned with dancelike movements with their hands.
As they return to classrooms, my new friend David
breaks away to greet and hug me. Alice
initiates a hug and he responds

most happily, then heeds his teacher's call
to join his classmates.

When they have all gone,
Aminda takes us to the clinic (same
building) where we meet the nurse, a Quaker
who, in essence, gives three hours a day here,
working fulltime in a hospital, too.
The doctor, small and almost childlike in
his fervency, is non-Quaker but surely
Friendly. He gives two hours a day here, and works
fulltime in pediatrics in a large hospital.
He speaks so fast we wouldn't understand
a thing if Aminda didn't slow him down,
repeating slowly his most cogent points.
Children suffer stomach problems often—
almost certainly the water is to blame:
few people can afford the bottled kind.
As word about the clinic spreads, they see
more patients all the time. The clinic lacks—
oh, nearly everything. Beseechingly
he tells what's needed most, maybe thinking
we can give or attract the modest money needed.
We thank him for his time, and tell him we
can promise nothing but will try our best.

While we were in the clinic, the children ate
their lunches. Dismissed, they frolic on the playground.
Now that we've been properly introduced
they come to hug us. David asks if he
can try my hat (a straw I bought in Costa
Rica). I lend it to him, suggesting that
he let his friends try it, too. They prance
around (I hope not imitating me!)
the hat sliding over the eyes of some.
I notice suddenly that I have heard

no quarrels on this playground. One boy shows
us all the toys he carries in his pockets,
the kinds of things one finds in Crackerjacks.
Alice has a finger puppet in
her purse, a wobbly yellow rubber monster
always ready to distract a restless
child on trains, in restaurants, in Meeting.
Now she mounts a short comedy.
The children are delighted. She could stay
forever here and never lack an audience.

MONDAY EVENING

Our afternoon siesta and a game
of balloon football in the living room
with Aminda's son and daughter have revived
us for another spell at church. Aminda
has told us we will eat a *tipica cena*
but both of us feel just enough unease
in our digestive tracts to make us decline
(*con cortesia apropiada,* we hope) the food
we're offered. At least as many people here
tonight as yesterday, with music from
the latin-jazzy combo, children running
everywhere, the women (some with infants
nursing) gathered for supper around tables
in one of the larger classrooms.

                          Likely, the men
have eaten before we came, for I am led
to the Meeting room for *el Grupo de Caballeros.*
Singing (accompanied by two guitars)
praying, reading a psalm aloud with each
responsible for several verses. Now
their business meeting: planning a fund-raiser,
a potluck meal followed by a movie,
already chosen. I feel at home amid
this quiet Quaker talk—deferential
but insistent, boundless. Each consults
his calendar repeatedly. At last
but suddenly they reach unity
(Friendlier than consensus) on the points
they have discussed. They shake hands, each
with everyone, and help me practice Spanish
conversation, speaking slowly, listening
carefully. The women wander in

and children run the aisles, unscolded, free.
We slowly make our way outside, conversing
all the while, and stand in the half-dark
still talking. They will meet again on Wednesday
evening, but we'll be headed home by then.
They seem reluctant to part, even for
so short a time. A true community.

Maudiel collects his children, leads
us to his car (Aminda's gone already)
and asks us if we're ready for our *tipica*
cena. Honest, we say that we *no tengo*
hambre, but the children have been promised,
and we should eat, he says, at least *un poco.*
We don't protest, and half an hour later
find ourselves inside a Mister Donut (!)
ordering *enchiladas.* They look and taste
like *pupusas* except that these have crumbled egg
and cheese on top. I wonder if we'll ever
find tortillas anywhere as good
as those we've eaten in El Salvador?
The children pester Maudiel for sweets
and he indulges them. Alice and I
have both been struck with admiration
at how well parents and children connect:
love and humor rule their give and take.
Even teens appear to like their parents!

TUESDAY

Miguel and his brother Eduardo come to take
us out for lunch. When we refuse to state
a preference, they suggest, "Maybe pizza?"
We say that that will suit us fine. Miguel's
English trumps our Spanish. Glad to lose
that contest, we enjoy his guided tour
of San Salvador: the National University,
which they attend; Children's Hospital, where
the Friends Clinic doctor works; several
beautiful parks; the U.S. Embassy,
maybe bigger overall than any
other institution here. We end
the tour at a shopping center such as one
might find near any prosperous city in
the U.S., except that the parking lot
provides the shade of many splendid trees.
Buildings two-and-three stories high
faced on every side by wide arcades
with broad stairways between the buildings. We
regret to recognize most names and logos
on the shops, including PIZZA HUT,
our destination.
                        After lunch, we drive
to the Quaker church. Eduardo leaves us there,
and soon we're joined by Douglas and Aminda.
Miguel's keyboard joins Douglas's guitar
in Aminda's trunk.
                        On the road again,
Aminda driving. She may have learned to drive
in the same accelerated course as Lidia,
but this is a four-lane highway. Settling back,
relaxed, we try to absorb the countryside

that flashes by: mountains, tiny towns,
and trees as varied as those we saw in Costa Rica.
Miguel and Douglas stick to English mostly,
though keeping Aminda posted on our questions
so she can help with answers.

.   A sudden roadblock
stops our progress. *Policias* carefully check
Aminda's papers and the license plates,
both front and rear, and ask our purpose and
our destination.

                    Under way again,
Miguel explains that drivers high on drugs
or alcohol immediately have
their cars expropriated, not to be
returned unless the proper palms are greased.
In Costa Rica we hardly ever saw police,
but here, especially in San Salvador,
either police or army units are
ubiquitous. No. demonstration stands
a chance of getting started. During the war,
we're told, this part of the country switched from one
allegiance to another often, and both
parties brutalized the population,
murdering many. Would the war have worn
so long or been so brutal if we had kept
our arms out of it and not trained
torturers (as we are doing still)
in the School of the Americas?

                            An hour later
we turn from the highway to a rutted road
that climbs the foothills of the mountains we
have been admiring. Dust envelops us
and trails behind. Twenty minutes later

we reach La Reina, a town of several thousand
people. Maudiel's parents live
here, and keep a shop that fronts their modest home.
(The *tienda* stocks such miscellany as
insecticides, sodas, candies, ice
cream and slush cones, and probably
much more, though these are what are sold
while we're around.) We're introduced to Madre
(stocky, brown and beaming) and to Padre
(slender, gray, and smiling). Behind the shop
a room that's roofed but open on the sides
contains two picnic tables, chairs, a clay
stove with a wood fire, a young macaw,
a dog, a rooster, hens (the fearless chickens
wander in and out at will) and two
mourning doves in a large cage, mumbling
woe. The stove sends up a plume of smoke
that slides below the roof till it escapes
along the open sides.

                    Miguel goes out
to fetch his keyboard, Douglas his guitar.
After tuning up, they start to play
a hymn, and Padre tilts his head to listen,
waves his hands to set a different rhythm,
sings along. Aminda gets us water
sealed in plastic pouches, and leads us to
the bathroom (modern plumbing) in the closed
space behind us. Madre and Padre take
the half-grown *loro* from his perch now
and then, encourage him to talk (no luck)
kiss him on the beak, and feed him pieces
of tortilla. Madre mixes tortillas
and fries a few on top of the clay stove
to feed the dog.

Aminda asks Alice and me
to come with her on visits in the town.
Miguel accompanies us, perhaps so Douglas
can have some private time with his *abuelos.*
First is Sister Alice, who is charmed
to meet another Alice (I think of little
David at the school). A handsome
brick house. Across the front a large room
with iron grilles instead of glass in windows.
In back of this, closed rooms on both
sides with a small garden-court between,
and in the court a cistern, fed with rain
runoff from the red tile roof. This room
has rattan furniture with cushions on
the chairs and colorful hangings on the walls.
I'd like to live in such an open house.
As we sit chatting, we are joined by Alice's
esposo, who smells pleasantly of horse
and leather. He joins the smalltalk, Bible-reading,
prayer.

Next we meet an old *senora*
(once a Jew but now a Quaker, she
has been to Israel and may have lived there).
Her daughter lives with her, or maybe the other
way around. Perhaps because my ennui
shows, Miguel inquires if I would like
to go with him when he returns to practice
songs with Douglas. Perhaps too eagerly
for courtesy, I say I will. Walking
back, we see a busy open market,
perhaps a fair, for there is lively music,
dancing, a carousel. Fat Tuesday
not till next week, but Miguel believes
this is a Catholic festival. When we

get back, Miguel and Douglas practice—Padre
helping choose the hymns and singing them.
Madre cooks some kind of meat on top
of the stove, fries perhaps the best of the best
tortillas I have ever eaten—thick
and crispy. Wrapped around the juicy meat
with salsa, they make a most delicious meal.

The Quaker church here is the oldest in
El Salvador, founded in 1926.
A large Meeting room with wooden pews.
A stage with lectern. Bare of ornament
but with one side that opens on a garden,
no glass to cut us off from natural scents
and trilling crickets—bird songs, too, at first.
Miguel and Douglas play and sing, and soon
the church resounds with celebrating voices.
Douglas delivers a short homily,
not spell-binding like his uncle, but
he keeps my full attention fixed (no easy
art with Spanish speech). Another hymn.
Aminda introduces us, then speaks
about the power of parents, pointing out
her in-laws and their shaping Maudiel
to be a model husband, father, son.
She also speaks about her own parents,
how they sacrificed for her and how
much gratitude she feels. Our Heavenly Father
and the Son He gave to save us from ourselves...
and here my mind begins to wander, not
aware how time is flying till I sense
the congregation gathering like the one
in Soyapango Sunday. Here, as there,
they rise and move to the open space between
the stage and pews, and kneel and pray together.
Miguel and Douglas join them, looking askance

at Alice and me as if to ask why we
alone of all that gathering keep our seats.
"Because the Spirit has not moved us," we
could say.

        Miguel will later ask me, "What
do you *do* in your Meeting? Is it true
that no one speaks and there's no music?"
I tell him, "People speak if they are led
to speak and sing if the Spirit moves them to sing.
Otherwise we wait in the Silence."

                                 He
appears to find this strange beyond belief,
and I begin to wonder at it, too:
that I have found a home and welcome there!

WEDNESDAY

We have a chunk of time to spend before
Mauricio Hernandez takes us to the airport.
Herman Ernesto, whom we have met but not
become acquainted with, has offered us
his hospitality till then, and we
are grateful for his fluent English.
We meet his wife (a Quaker-quiet Rita
Moreno) and their two wee children (dark,
with lively eyes and winning ways). Then
a guided tour of their home, larger than
most other homes we've seen in Soyapango,
but sparely furnished. Herman managed a store
in Cambridge, Mass. for several years, and saved
enough to buy this house. His children, born
in the U.S., have dual citizenship
but seem to speak no English. Herman says
he went to Cambridge Meeting sometimes, but found
it didn't meet his need:

                         "Christ was un-
welcome there," he says. "Is your Meeting
like that?" he asks. We say that members of
our Meeting run the gamut from atheists
to those who find their center in Jesus. He asks,
"And you? Have you accepted Christ as Savior?"

Alice finds her reticence a refuge.

"Jesus lives in my imagination,"
I say, "and helps me when I pray to Him,
but, no, I don't believe He'll save me from sin:
that is my responsibility, and I

confess that often I'm not equal to
the task."

Herman sadly shakes his head.
"Have you tried inviting Jesus in?
He's not like the Other One who barges in
unasked. No, Jesus is polite and waits
to be invited. If you ask Him, though,
and with an open heart, He'll enter in
and change your lives for you. You'll know such joy
as only those who harbor Him can know."

Suddenly, I suspect that Herman has
been asked to try what altar-calls in Spanish
haven't done: to convert us to the faith
that animates this good community
of Friends, a faith I honor and admire
but doubt will ever find a home in me.

"After I was saved," says Herman, "I
became a missionary. The good Gospel
news overflowed my spirit. I had
to share it with everyone. I'm thinking now
of going to the U.S. again,
soon, to learn Cambodian so I
can be a missionary in Cambodia."

His wife, with children clinging shyly to
her skirt, brings tea and coffee. I notice now
her bulging middle (maybe six months
along?) and think that missionary zeal
may have its prudent side.

We pass an hour
or so exchanging experiences of one
another's countries. When Mauricio

arrives to take us to the airport, Herman
writes his name, address, and phone number
down for us, and urges us again
to ask Jesus to enter our hearts. "Please write or call
me when it happens. I'll share the happy news
with all your friends here."

                                    I want to tell
him, "We're from Minnesota, and couldn't ask
Him in until our hearts are spotless and all
their contents in perfect order." But jokes about
salvation wouldn't do. My making one,
even in my head, reveals the lack
in me of any talent for belief.

Yet again I find myself no match
for sin: envy of Herman's piety
floods my spirit.
                         Christ Jesus, please
come in and light my dark, disordered heart.

But Jesus knows there is no room for him
at this too busy wayside inn, my heart.

FLYING HOME

The country disappears beneath us, concealed
by clouds. Already my experience there
begins to fade as I anticipate
arriving home to snow and blustery winds.
Please help me keep those new-found Friends alive
in memory. They've wakened possibilities
of faith and service I'd be loath to lose.

Our seatmate, in his sixties, large and loud,
a US citizen who says he lives
most of the year in Salvador. His wife
is Salvadoran. Now retired, he worked
till recently for the US government
in Salvador. I wish that I could quell
my suspicion that he added to the woe
the country suffered in the war. He has
opinions and means for us to share
as many as he can impose on us.

I'm glad we saw the country for ourselves,
and not just tourist traps. Perhaps the Friends
gave us a partial notion of the place,
but five days with them revealed more truth
than we could find in a year in enclaves
of retired Americans. Or do I fool
myself? How much did I misunderstand
when Maudiel, Aminda, Alice and I
blundered through our stumbling conversations?
But there's that subtle sense we get of other
folks that language doesn't mediate.
I mean to trust my happy memories.

BEING WANTED

SOMEONE HERE TO SEE YOU, MARYANN.
SAYS HE KNEW YOU LONG AGO.

                    Long
enough ago and I may remember him.
Who is it? My vision is so bad I can't
recognize you nurses, let alone
a person I haven't seen in a long time.

I'm Darrell Montgomery. You were my
Sunday School and Bible School teacher
back in the 1930s. I don't expect
that you remember me, but I have thought
of you often over the years, and want
at last to thank you. Jesus lives for me
because you told his stories well.

                    Darrell WHO?
My hearing's near as bad as my vision. You'll have
to talk louder.

              DARRELL MONTGOMERY.
WE LIVED KITTYCORNER FROM THE BASS
LAKE SCHOOL.

    Oh, Montgomery! You
and your sister went to the Bass Lake Church, and I
taught you in the Sunday School. You'd moved
before I taught the Bass Lake School, I think.
I remember all your family.

All of you were ever so polite.
I told Mother once that you were the most
polite family in the neighborhood,
and she said that was a good thing because
you weren't likely ever to be so rich
you wouldn't need good manners. Once I tried
to get your folks to sign a petition to keep
the Bass Lake Resort from serving beer.
Your father very nicely asked if I
had got my brothers to sign, and when I said
I hadn't, he said that he would wait
till they had signed. In other words, he meant
not to sign it, and meant for me to mind
my own business, but he was so polite
I couldn't take offense. My brothers were
the biggest drinkers in the neighborhood
The Resort could have stayed in business just
with their patronage. They'd come home drunk
at all hours, but mostly in the early
morning. Mother sometimes scolded them,
but she could see no wrong in anything
they did, really. They were good farmers,
she said, and that was true. Their children own
most all the land around the Lake these days,
and that's because their fathers did so well.
Big noisy fellows, always trying
to embarrass me. They got their natures from
our mother. I was like my father, small
and quiet, but my father died when I
was just a girl. I was alone among
those noisy, grasping people half my life.
The only man that ever courted me
was Catholic, and poor besides, a farmhand.

Mother said he only wanted me
to get some land, and maybe she was right.
My brothers scared him off, or paid him off,
and no one ever asked me out again.
Mother didn't mind that Bob married
Catholic and reared a brood of big noisy
Catholic kids. She let me go to college
finally—well, just the Normal School
so I could teach in country schools—but when
she died I finally got away from them.
I taught for thirty years and luckily
I have a little pension to flesh out
my Social Security. In her will,
Mother said that since she'd paid for me
to go to college, I had got my share,
so all three farms went to my two brothers.
Imagine! One year in Normal School—
it must have cost her all of fifty dollars!
I clerked in the 5 & dime whenever I
was not in class. Now, you won't mind, I hope,
if I ask again just who you are? I can't
remember anything except it's far
back in time.

   I'M DARRELL MONTGOMERY.
I WAS VISITING MY AUNT, WHO HAS A ROOM
UPSTAIRS, AND SHE REMINDED ME THAT YOU
ARE HERE.

   And who might she be—your aunt,
I mean?

   HER NAME IS EDNA FOY.

Oh, yes, Edna Foy. She's
the only one in here that's older than I,
but she gets lots of visitors. I guess
she had a dozen kids and each of them
a dozen more, and they have not forgot
her. My brothers died a long time ago,
and none of their children ever come
to visit. Some of the children I taught
stop in, but they are always in a hurry.
I sometimes think not even God wants me,
or else He'd let me die and be with Him.

OLD DOG DEATH

Last night I sweat and shook and dreamed
of Old Dog Death. His canines gleamed
in dripping, silent jaws. I deemed
it wise to wake at once. When I
awoke, he slept. I'll let him lie.
He'll do as much for me by and by.

DAVID LANGWORTHY · 188

A DOXOLOGY, OF SORTS

To praise You from Whom all blessings flow
(all tempests, quakes and ills, also)
I praise Your son, who lights my way
if I but ask his help each day.

For Jesus, shining, shows me how
to live within a world of woe
and love the work of Your hands,
even that which no one understands.

Are earthquakes, storms and sufferings meant
to stretch us to our full extent?
Blessings, unalloyed, may keep
us basking on the edge of sleep,

but troubles try us and so wake
our nodding souls to wonder, shake
us from complacency to awe,
making us question natural law.

When babies, born with fell disease,
die soon but hard; or pheasants freeze
in sleety winter storms; or rumbling
quakes and slides send structures tumbling

to crush the startled folk within;
or sparrows fall (not into sin)
how can it help that Your eye
is on them as they sorely die?

Reluctant to accept our own
comeuppance, how can we condone
the suffering of innocents?
Is it but Your incompetence

from which such unfair sufferings rise
to cloud the glory of Your skies?
Are You a Power that errs sometimes,
a pattern for our human crimes?

How the faithful Son of Man
did love You, bumbling Artisan!
Though loath to taste the bitter cup,
he yielded, and drank it up.

If we could love, as Jesus did,
Your whole flawed creation, we'd
know better what we need to do
so that our deeds might honor You.

But we, or most of us, fall short:
we love ourselves, and our sort,
but not our enemies (or those
we fancy may *become* our foes).

We love Your natural world as long
as it inspires a blithesome song,
but we can surely do without
a lengthy, desiccating drought!

Be careful how You end one, though,
for either mounting drifts of snow
or more than sweet and gentle rain
and we will certainly complain!

Christ Jesus, light us up within
to help us overcome the sin
of often wanting more or less
than God has freely given us.

Help us not confuse Nature's
gifts with what our social structures
all too bounteously yield to some
while putting others on the bum.

And I, a frequent hypocrite,
most especially need your light
to help me live what I believe,
embracing all Your world with love.

VARIATIONS ON
A NEGATIVE

Lao-tsu argued that nothingness is useful,
but nothing makes no sense to me.
While I did not ask to be born,
neither did I ask not to be born;
and though I did not make this world
that I did not ask (not) to be born into,
it's no worse than no world I could make
and far better than no world at all.
In short, I would not rather not be,
not nowhere.
I'd rather be ashes or worms and weeds
than nothing. Besides, nothing is not optional.

ON LOOKING DOWN
TO SEE THE SUN

When I once stared too boldly at the sun,
to chasten me all nature blurred
to a blazing darkness. I knew no word
to sound those deeps, and thought I was undone.

Today I happened to see the sun afloat
in a wrinkled puddle where August rain
had spilled from the ruts in a country lane.
It rode the ripples there like a waiting boat.

POSTCARD TO
MARY HARRIS

Hearing today of the California coast
lashed by rain, cliffs crumbling again
into the sea, we prayed for you, Mary; recalled
climbing the steep, narrow path (once
a road that tumbled long ago to the beach)
from your modest cottage to our car.
You carried your eighty years as gaily as we
remembered our forty-five years' friendship.
We hope to see you there again, unbowed
as ever, still painting, still planning
peace and working to bring it near as here.
After a storm, you are one of sundry
suns filling the broken world with light.

OAK CENTER GENERAL STORE & FOLK FORUM

Beside the door a large hand-lettered
sign: LIVE MUSIC TODAY. Behind
the building, draft horses, cattle, hogs
and poultry fufill the sign's promise and add
a medley of smells to their music and to the wood
smoke in the air. Step through the door and back
a hundred years. Goods in bins and barrels
lift aromas in the air to match
the green smell of potting plants: tomatoes,
flowers, herbs, and vegetables. Garden tools
and other tools are on display. The shelves
hold makings for meals instead of readymades.
Behind the counter, Susan greets you, a smile
lighting up her long weary face;
if you haven't paid already, she accepts
your $5 (or if you are a child
you get in free). In back, a spacious room
dominated by a woodburning range,
where steaming kettles wait for tea-making.
Nearby, a table offers empty mugs
and pumppots full of several blends of coffee,
with a basket for your money. Here
the shelves hold books—some fiction, but more on health,
the environment, social action, history.
The higher shelves display home-canned fruit
and vegetables, winter meals for the family,
whose smallest members may come dashing by
in costumes or in as nearly nothing as
they dare. People stand about chatting
or sink into the rump-sprung couch or easy

chairs and rockers. Behind this room a wide
steep single flight of wooden stairs
takes you through popcorn-scented air to the room
where folks gather in rows of folding chairs.
A counter offers popcorn, bottled drinks
(including beer) and monster oatmeal cookies.
Angled to form an alcove, another counter
displays CDs of today's musicians, and
a basket labeled: DONATIONS. Behind is a door
to the family's living space (of course they live
all over all this space, but like you they need
some privacy sometimes). A small, shallow
stage (where community dramas have unfolded)
holds a grand piano, drums, guitars,
microphones and music stands and chairs.
The general hubbub begins to fade
as Steven mounts the stage. Like Susan he
looks bone-weary, but as he gets the crowd's
attention, his shoulders lift and he begins
his customary speech: the earth is on
the verge of ruin, but is gloriously
worth saving: here are things that we can do
to help it last another year or two.
Enlivened by his own wit and wisdom,
Steven works the crowd and asks for their
suggestions, news. A basset hound
may join him on the stage, will certainly
at some point in the day's performance join
the musicians, maybe sample what they're drinking.
The basset is a favorite of the crowd,
and she will work them for cookie crumbs and spilled
popcorn as the music plays. At last
Steven, sensing the crowd's accumulating
restlessness, provides today's performers
with warm and welcoming words, and they emerge

from the family apartment, where they've likely
enjoyed a hearty home-cooked meal.
Sometime today they'll tell why they have come
from grander venues around the world to this
tiny village far from any city,
to this tiny unpretentious hall:
they love Susan, Steven, all the family
and all they stand for; and relish the wild
enthusiasm you and your friends provide.

PREMATURE FAREWELL

How can I have lived
so long
and done so little that matters,
yet had so good a time
so far?
Will I be chastened before
I die
to expiate my smug
content?
Though seldom dejected or bored
with life
since childhood's dependency,
I dread
the onset of ennui more than
death
or any fell disease—
less,
however, than loneliness:
the deeper
I know my neighbors, the fuller
I live.

So long, dear world. So far, I die
content with life. I dread death less
the deeper I live.

PART FIVE

Fables

THE FROG WHO WOULD
BE PRESIDENT

A frog decided he would run
for President. "Anyone
who puffs himself as much as I,
and peers so piously at high
ideals while splashing through the mud,
and spreads his mouth in such a broad
mendacious grin, and stoutly spouts
the same few formulae without
getting sick on them—well, who
that has such talents can eschew
the muck and muddle of campaigning?"
he croaked. Just then it started raining,
and other creatures scrambled for shelter.
The frog sat steadfast amid the welter,
pleased to see his puddle spread.
"I take this as a sign," he said,
"that Heaven itself approves my plan,
enlarging thus my small domain.
Perhaps I only have to wait
and God will make me Chief of State."

A heron that was standing near,
one leg tucked up beside her rear,
had heard with scorn the froggy's gab.
Censoriously she tried to stab
the frog, but as she struck, a sneer
deformed her beak. She couldn't spear
with it, but found its twist a great
shape for political debate.
"*You* run for President!
Your squatting posture says it's bent

to stay, won't even let you *stand*
for office. No doubt you're underhand
enough for politics; however,
your extremities were never
meant to steer the Ship of State:
you, Sir, are invertebrate!
Although a President may be
as brainless as a hopping flea,
he can't be spineless except before
the pros and profiteers of war.
Frogs swim, they hop, they bask in the sun,
but never has a froggy *run.*"
The heron's sneer grew so complex
posing these quibbles, she was vexed
to find her beak stuck in a log,
having missed the lucky frog.
Seeing which, the frog decamped,
his campaign fever scarcely damped.
He hopped away to the river's brink
and paused awhile thereon to think.
A northern pike swam by and spotted
him as thoughtfully he squatted.
"Such contemplation as I see
on yonder lowly brow may be
combined with absent-mindedness,"
the pike surmised. "I find success
rewards a patient appetite
more times than not. I'll wait polite-
ly here, and maybe he will leap
directly down my throat while deep
in thought."
                Imagine Pike's dismay
when Frog stood upright. "Let us pray,"

the candidate began, "in school;
for all agree that as a rule
we seldom, if ever, meet with prayer
in the marketplace or anywhere
like that." The frog toppled then
and rested gasping; rose again
to speak but promptly fell. Persistence
often carries one the distance
one intends to go, and so
it was with Frog, who learned to throw
his weight as he must do to stand
erect throughout a boldly bland
freshly canned oration.
                       Pike,
admiring Frog's workmanlike
approach, smothered her regret
at losing supper. A cool coquette,
she flapped her fins and bubbled bravos,
offered all her saved centavos
to back him in his bold ambition,
coyly hinted at coition
should he be so inclined—in short,
to ride his coattails into court
was her design.
                   "My First Lady,"
Frog replied, bowing. Afraid she
might discern his double-meaning
or, worse, assume an overweening
role in his campaign, he took
her money, promising to book
her for his Cabinet, then blew
a kiss to her as he withdrew.

Although no scandal yet besmeared
his name, the frog then disappeared—
unless, of course, one trusts the rumor
(but surely this is someone's humor?)
that he is one of those now stumping
across our glutted nation, dumping
loads of predigested fears
and promises in voter's ears.

THE FRENCH POODLE AND THE HEINZ DOG

"What I wants to nose,"
said French Poodle, "is how
a Heinz dog can suppose
his lowbrow bowwow
attracts or frightens me."
Lips curled, she sniffed
and stared up at a tree-
top. Although he was miffed,
the mutt whose yard she stood in
offered his paw.
"My name, madame, is Goodwin.
A certain *je ne sais quois*
about you piques my interest.
Clearly you presume
that humble origin must
earn disdain. *La plume
de ma tante* of course is prose.
But then, *le monocle
de mon oncle's* a *quelque chose*.
This family chronicle
was interrupted by
French Poodle's chortle,
a sound to mortify
a common canine mortal.
But Goodwin, humble birth
aside, was far from common.
Rejoiced by Poodle's mirth
he capered: starting from an
amble 'round the bitch
with nose asnuffle, his pace

increased to such a pitch
and introduced such grace-
ful leaps and twists that she
was quite bowled over
by him. What though he
was just a common Rover?
Such wit and *joie de vivre*
as he possessed she seldom
met with. "I'm naïve,
perhaps," she coyly told him,
"but anyway I find
your sweet attentions welcome."
And I may be thin-skinned,"
the mutt replied, "but nonetheless
your change of heart comes late,
and gladly I confess
that giving you the gate
is all I wish. Good day,
madame." He bowed most courtly
and, sauntering away,
was napping shortly.

Moral:
Pride goes before a fall,
and tripping it promotes morale.

NOTES

Till the Cows Came Home: "the township's central gossip"—
the events of the this poem date to a time when each
small town had its own telephone company with a
Central operator who knew and shared everybody's
business. As a college student I called home collect
once and Mrs. McMonagle scolded me, "Have you
run out of money already, young man?"

Enough's Enough: When my uncle Mark tricked Aunt Julia
once this way, she told the story to Mother, who had
called to make sure they got home alright. This poem
is based on Julia's telling the story later at family dinners.
The events of the story occurred in the 1940s when
farmers lucky enough to have electricity turned on their
yardlights only as needed. Though there are fewer
farmsteads in the Midwest nowadays, each one has at
least one yardlight shining throughout the night.

Vivid Ghosts: These poems grew from my experiences as a
conscientious objector during the Korean War. My
CO status was based on conscience only, not religion,
but in the Army medical service I first met Quakers,
whose examples stuck in my memory, eventually
winning me to their practice.

On the Road: "idle acres"—In the 1960-70s, to help control
the overproduction of corn, farmland was kept from
production and called "idle acres".

BVG